Wha

1,39

SMALL BATCH

Small Batch

Local, Organic, and Sustainable Church

C. Andrew Doyle

Copyright © 2016 by C. Andrew Doyle.

Library of Congress Control Number:		2016907814
ISBN:	Hardcover	978-1-5245-0015-3
	Softcover	978-1-5245-0016-0
	eBook	978-1-5245-0014-6

All rights reserved. No part of this book may be reproduced or transmitted in any form or by any means, electronic or mechanical, including photocopying, recording, or by any information storage and retrieval system, without permission in writing from the copyright owner.

Any people depicted in stock imagery provided by Thinkstock are models, and such images are being used for illustrative purposes only. Certain stock imagery © Thinkstock.

Print information available on the last page

Rev. date: 05/16/2016

To order additional copies of this book, contact:
Xlibris
1-888-795-4274
www.Xlibris.com
Orders@Xlibris.com
550319

Contents

Acknowledgments ix
Introduction xi
Foreword: Moon Launch xiii

Chapter 1: The Shift 1
Chapter 2: From Opaque History to Autopoetic Mission 11
Chapter 3: Renewed Mission Field 26
Chapter 4: The Birth of Vitality and Mission Amplification 38
Chapter 5: Church and the Continuum of Mission 50
Chapter 6: Emerging Small Batch Communities and Their Values 63
Chapter 7: A Budding Missiology 79
Chapter 8: Small Batch Leadership 96
Chapter 9: Starting Your Small Batch Community 103
Chapter 10: Three From The Beginning 111
Chapter 11: Frequently Asked Questions 120
Chapter 12: Communities of Inspiration 125
Chapter 13: Let There Be No Misunderstanding 127

About the Author 139
Endnotes 141

If it is of the spirit
we will see it all around us,
springing up in a variety of places.
—Mariann Budde

In order to find the center
you have to go to the margins.
—Mark Beckwith

Acknowledgments

The amazing thing about this book is the incredible people undertaking incredible missional ministries against huge oppositional forces. They have found, scrounged together, taped, glued, and knit communities together through their own investment of time and resources. I am grateful that each person took the time to share with me his or her story, thoughts, learning, and time. This book is not possible without the firsthand accounts of people doing amazing gospel work. They shared e-mails and many had phone conversations.

Let me thank Paul Skeith, Emily Scott, Scott Claasen, Katie Nakamura Rengers, David Peters, Oliver Glass, Andy Parker, Sara Shisler Goff, Bob Leopold, Bob Lowry, Kerlin Richter, Steve Kinney, Debbie Allensworth, Jim Liberatore, Angie Thurman, Casper de Kutie, Angie Thurman, and Bertie Pearson. This book is a far better contribution to the discussion of the future of the church because these people gave me a good amount of their time and shared their story. As a bishop I am always aware that what makes ministry fantastic is the gift to work with the people you have read about in this book.

I am grateful for a tremendous staff. Canon Kai Ryan's introduction is a wonderful challenge to the church to be tenacious and undaunted in our courageous missionary efforts. Canon John Newton helped with a good bit of reflection on my thoughts and helped me to put a great deal on paper. We then invited our team (Bishops Dena Harrison and Jeff Fisher and Canon Mary MacGregor) to reflect and give us feedback on direction. Our thoughts are the collection of over one hundred years of congregational experience. Wisdom always come from sharing and conversation. I am blessed to have wonderful conversation partners.

All of this makes me want to be a better minister and to make room for others to follow in their footsteps, which I think are the footsteps of Jesus. The church has much to learn as it enters the wilderness of a new missionary age. I am grateful for a Moses generation who are leading us bravely into God's intended future.

Introduction

When I was in seminary, like many folks, I studied Martin Luther, who is best known for his ninety-five theses; however, I stumbled upon a little known work, *On The Babylonian Captivity of the Church*.[1] The overall work is Luther's examination of the sacraments. At the time, people only received the bread at the Eucharist. Luther advocated for the restoring of the cup to the laity so they could receive communion in both kinds. The proposition is that the sacraments and the church itself are held captive by the church's structures, just as King Nebuchadnezzar besieged and enslaved the Jews in 528 and held them captive in Babylon. In complete Luther-esque style, using plenty of colorful comparisons, Luther offers that the church may not itself possess the dream of God. If this is the case, it needs to be reformed.

Luther would expand this criticism of the church to all facets of its ministry. In many ways, Luther, like all the reformers, felt the church had lost its way. It had become about church more than the mission of Christ in the world. The great reform moved people to read the Bible, create their own forms of religion, and become spiritual pilgrims on their own. The reformers and their followers realized the church was not bound to the hierarchy and economic forms of the day. They freed it to explore new life.

The church has since then believed that ministry—and the ministry of the sacrament of the Eucharist—was an important and key ingredient to Christian community. Certainly this is true in the Anglican tradition. So important is this reality that, during World War II, Florence Li Tim-Oi, a Chinese woman, was ordained by The Right Reverend Ronald Hall, Bishop of Victoria, Hong Kong, in 1944. He did this because the Japanese invasion caused the men to flee. The Reverend Li Tim-Oi went into the occupied territory to minister and celebrate the sacrament for the church members left behind. We understand that the sacrament is part of what it means to be an Anglican community.

No denomination today would fault the reformers for their work. Yet like the Roman Catholics of Luther's day, we have imprisoned the mission because of our love of doing church and worshipping in church buildings. And we are inwardly fed by ministry focused on those who are members. We are stuck. It has been difficult for us to imagine doing mission work outside of a particular economic model, a one priest–one church model.

As we begin to think about sending out people to start small batch communities, communities focusing on ministry with a particular group, we must face the fact that the mission will not be very sustainable if we have to provide full-time clergy for each one. This is exactly the problem.

Our mission, our ability to start new communities, cannot be dictated by the economics of the situation, nor the training or any of the structural pieces that get in the way. We must, at the end, free the church from its Babylonian captivity by a modern structure that no longer serves the mission. Moreover, like Bishop Hall, we must use all means necessary to create our sacramental communities.

This is so key as we think about moving to a distributive system of church mission with a multiplication of small batch communities that are networked with churches. So let us envision a free mission supported by the church that roots itself around a table set in the world.

Foreword

Moon Launch

On May 25, 1961, President John F. Kennedy delivered a now-famous speech where he challenged America to put a man on the moon before the end of the decade. What Kennedy proposed was radical, a sign of the changing world and emerging scientific and human capacities. The task exceeded human knowledge. America succeeded, in part, because of the ingenuity and courage of astronauts. NASA gave the astronauts their best training. They learned how to make a home in a small space capsule. They learned countdown procedures, plans and simulations for correcting errors, and all of the details of their capsules, modules, and landing gear. Trial runs proceeded in their newfangled space suits. All was top of the line. But there was one experience beyond any purchase price or human power to produce, one thing we might consider essential. Their training lacked actual time in space.

Astronaut training could not really prepare men or women for the experience of being 239,000 miles beyond the Earth. It could not offer a place to practice the totality of the experience of stepping out onto the surface of the moon or the utter loneliness of handling a disaster during the hours when Mission Control was out of range. Scientists could not even duplicate the conditions of space. Astronauts had to enter the foreign reality in charge of expensive missions and perform tasks on which their lives depended, without ever having experienced space itself. Until repeated space travel expanded human comprehension of space conditions, every astronaut set out with that basic training deficiency, a lack of time in space.

To compensate, they took on their assignments with courage, trust, and a good deal of bravado.

What does it take to lead in times of transition? The answer is that same crazy combination of courage, trust, and audacity. This I know for the Bible tells us so. Back in the day, the Lord was working through Israel's leadership dilemma. Samuel, Saul, or David? None were especially well-prepared to lead the people of Israel in the topsy-turvy world in which they found themselves. Samuel's call came at the end of the age of the Judges, when Israel needed relief from the drunken and selfish exploits of Eli's sons. The tribes were hardly a unified people at that point. Samuel was just a boy when the Lord wrenched him out of his sleep. Samuel led like a prophet-judge. But history marched on. For the people of Israel to thrive in the unfolding age, they needed a new vision of community and leadership. Loosely connected tribes could not endure the pressures from more organized neighbors. So Israel demanded a king, and the Lord had Samuel anoint Saul, a Benjaminite from the least of the tribes, who was searching for lost donkeys when doused with Samuel's king-making oil. Saul led as he could, but he was beset by flaws, and the Philistines just wouldn't let up.

So God sent Samuel to anoint a ruddy-faced and handsome boy too small to stand up under the weight of Saul's armor. In their turn, Samuel, Saul, and David said yes when appointed to lead. Like the astronauts, each needed to have had his own share of courage and audacity to face the complicated challenges into which he stepped. However, none knew what that leadership or office would entail.

We serve with God in a world and a church undergoing radical renovation. When the church undertakes ministry in this new millennia, we're a little like NASA in its early days. We stand in the middle of the programs and sacramental life of a mid-twentieth-century church and know God intends a healthy and thriving future church. It's like we stand on terra firma and gaze at the stars. We know we want to get to that future church, but we have little sense of how. And I don't think Google maps will help us! We struggle to grasp the nature of the world of the future and the church that God's mission there requires.

Changing at a rapid pace, our world needs an adaptive church. Brave souls have taken early adaptive steps, establishing alternative recruiting and training programs for lay and ordained leaders, experimenting with partnerships in our communities, and gathering communities for worship, fellowship, and service outside our traditional parish walls. Their efforts—both successes and failures—remind us that we can count on God's abundant provision to sustain the life of the church in this transitional time. But in truth we see the future church like we see in a mirror dimly.

Grasping what will work in the future church is a little like space travel. You can't experience it until you experience it. We live in a VUCA (volatile, uncertain, complex, and ambiguous) world, to use an acronym coined by the US Military War College and used by the futurist Bob Johansen and Bishop Doyle. That is the world in which we live, in which we do ministry. We have no choice. A VUCA world requires a VUCA-adaptive church, one that is visionary, understanding, clear, and agile. The ministry of a VUCA-adaptive church requires adaptive visionary leaders ready to go out and gain clarity and understanding by doing.

Most of us have been habituated in and for a church of a certain sort, designed to share the gospel in a certain environment, one that is stable, simple, and predictable. Or if not simple, it's at least a manageable level of complexity. We are native in the attractional style of the church. We've adopted the leadership practices of a "build it and they will come (and be saved)" church because that is all we know. We need the courage and audacity to adapt. It would be downright destructive to pretend otherwise.

God's work in the VUCA world needs a church that is missional, that is, courageous, flexible, diverse, and creative to its core. It's a church defined not by buildings and those inside them, but by relationships and engagement with those not yet in the embrace of Jesus and his body.

Today, scores of lay folk and clergy are adapting. We are like the members of the Greatest Generation who may have grown up without a phone in their home, yet we have learned to use iPads and Facebook to keep in touch with grandchildren and great-grandchildren.

Astronauts, even after dozens of space walks, will never be fully at home in space. We, those of us who love and lead the church today, in a similar way, will never be fully natural in the future church. How we engage in church now, however, impacts whether the future church will have leaders naturally adapted to the new environment. This part of our work resembles Samuel's much more than David's.

King David, coming where he does in the history of Israel, is born for leadership in a new age. You and I are like Samuel, leading God's people at a time of transition so the church can thrive in new ways in a world just now unfolding. Taking on the work of growing Episcopal Christians at home in the future church will not be for the weakhearted. We will have to stop seeing the adaptations of newer or younger leaders as mutations to be eradicated rather than the life-sustaining modifications they are. But their modifications will mean they will not be able to thrive in the church in which we are most comfortable. There will be, in a sense, no turning back.

Scientists (and science-fiction-ists) have long imagined that the real way to equip human beings for the future will be genetic modification. If genetically modified plants survive so well, why not humans? But consider the implications of genetic modification in human beings. In Polly Holyoke's novel for teenagers, *The Neptune Project*, Holyoke imagines a world in which the rise of the oceans and global political turmoil drive a community of scientists to conclude that they have to take radical steps if their children will have any future at all. They genetically modify their children so they could survive in an underwater world. By triggering the completion of the transformation, the parent-scientists free their children to live fully and freely underwater, but also limit them to their aqua world, a life into which their parents can never follow. In talking about the parents in her stories, Holyoke wrote,

> Of course it was a terrible choice and the world as they saw it had to be racing headlong into disaster or they never would have attempted something so desperate … The mother in the story is first and foremost a scientist on a mission and didn't really understand how wrenching it would be to give up her children.

As the church, we do pretty well at understanding grief and loss. We even know that God's healing includes death and loss, so we resist the temptation to avoid death at all costs. Such aptitude should equip us for the occasional gut-wrenching experience of letting go of our secret hope that those who follow will maintain our church in a form fully recognizable to us, one that is not recognizable to many of the Christians who have come before us. In order to serve God's mission, it's enormously more important that the unfolding world can recognize the future church as a vibrant community in which to encounter the living God than it is for us to recognize it as our own. Bishop Doyle has said, "We will continue in the apostle's teaching, fellowship, and the breaking of the bread but we will not be the church of yesteryear or a bygone era."

Today's adaptive leaders are migrating into a sending, missional outlook and habits. They minister as missional migrants rather than missional natives, trying hard to hold lightly favorite images of the way the church should be so it may become what God needs it to be. What we are invited to do is to intentionally disciple those who will mess up the church in which we are so comfortable. Mentoring them well will form them in ways that will make it hard for them to serve in the church as we know it.

Yet one day, with God's grace, we will be amazed at the natural ways in which another generation of leaders, missional natives, will intuitively but deeply orchestrate the interplay of technology, authenticity, and community in this new age with the essential living of "One Lord, One Faith, One Baptism."

In the sixties, those who brought America into space were motivated by the conviction that the goal to get to the moon was of real consequence, a potential life-and-death matter. The astronauts shared that belief, so they risked their lives to go where no one had gone before. Samuel faced a parade of Jesse's sons and the Lord's voice saying "This is not the king you are looking for" before marking David as God's own leader for the future Israel.

God himself has convicted us that we stand at a similar moment. Christ's work of reconciliation remains the world's constant life-and-death need, change what may.

—Reverend Canon Kai Ryan

Chapter 1

The Shift

What is happening in the system of the church is an organic paradigm shift. I first learned about paradigm shifts from The Right Reverend Claude E. Payne and his staff when I was a young priest. They wanted us to understand that we had to be part of shifting the church culture from maintenance to mission. We were the leaders responsible for helping the church make a paradigm shift.

Deeper reading led me to Thomas S. Kuhn's work. Recently a friend talked with me over coffee, reminding me of Kuhn and his landmark scientific essay, "The Structure of Scientific Revolution." It is now more than fifty years old. He is credited with popularizing the phrase "paradigm shift" and scientifically showing how shifts work within the scientific community.

Kuhn offers that revelation, creativity, and solutions to dilemmas come from the edges. Solutions to crises and paradigm shifts take shape outside the norm. They also take time and are hard to see while the shift is occurring; in fact, oftentimes you can't see them until they fully supplant the older paradigms.

Those who have the most to gain from a system staying the same will always sit in the choice seats, the "power broker seats," as Brené Brown would say. They have, after all, created the arena we must play in. They have supported and remained invested in its sustainability. The arena is that place where we make church happen. These are those individuals that Kuhn calls "the disciplinary matrix."[2] Within this matrix are the individuals who have accepted a certain set of theories about the paradigm. They are devoted to it, empowered by it, and often have authority within it. This is Brené Brown's arena. This is most of the denominational church today. Its boundaries make up the church property and buildings. It is separate from the world around it. Those who enter must play by the member's rules. It can be a particularly unwelcoming, inhospitable environment. It can seem like a world of a bygone era. We are completely invested in the disciplinary matrix of a past way of being church. All the church systems of hierarchies, committees, and commissions are imprisoned by the ideas that support and make this older way of being a Christian community work since the Victorian Age.

Some will disagree with me about this. I frequently hear that the parish church has worked for over a thousand years. Yet history is clearly on my side here. The way in which people have engaged in Christian community for the vast majority of history has not been through a church, as the Western parish leadership believes. Nevertheless our commission on ministries, seminaries, and leadership recruitment, church planting, and congregational growth strategies are all part of this present but past disciplinary matrix.

What I have learned is that, as the paradigm breaks down, those on the inside have the most to lose as the paradigm shifts. Their voices, power, and control will inevitably be lessened in the face of new revelations. As the arena, paradigm, or worldview shifts, these individuals begin to get louder. They try to shut down and manipulate the system to keep out the innovators, both early and midrange adopters.

Here is the amazing thing about the shift though. It needs the best part of the disciplinary matrix, which works most effectively when both the invested and the innovator stay in conversation on those areas of common and shared understanding. Incredible energy and creativity is generated in this contact through these linkages.

Unfortunately within the church, what has more often happened is that this friction has created either/or scenarios. When this happens, it removes the potential creative energy from the system and the essential DNA, tradition, learning, and stories that are important to all new movements. This means, if we harvest the power and energy already within the disciplinary matrix of our church system and leverage it with innovators, we will have a much stronger and healthier paradigm shift.

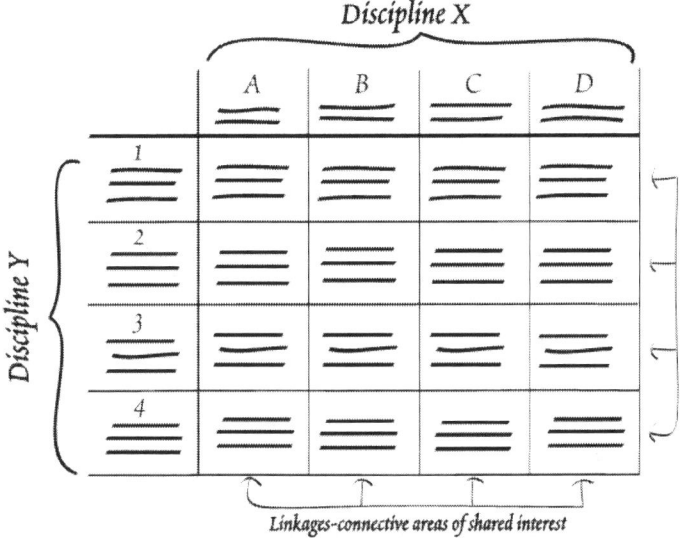
Linkages-connective areas of shared interest

Kuhn suggests, as a new paradigm and disciplinary matrix emerges, it becomes difficult for the two groups to converse, the old keepers of the paradigm and the new emerging innovators. He talks about a discipline X and discipline Y. (See chart.[3]) They begin to move apart and separate. There is an "incommensurability" between them. They actually both need one another, but as the shift occurs and power begins to be lessened, the voices go up, as do the attacks. They often tend to focus on and criticize those areas not commonly shared. Or they go after those areas where the creativity is most public. In doing this, it is easy to have the movement get focused on side issues and not the real work. Over the years, societal wars and cultural shifts have been one way the church's mission has been derailed by nonessential issues. Liturgical innovations have been another example of how contextual mission reform, which is very public, has become a way of focusing attention on the symptoms of shifts. This has happened for millennia and has been particularly troubling to Anglicans in our brief history. Reform churches have particular difficulty with future reforms.

In today's electronic age, those voices that would normally go unheard are now given more power and visibility via electronic and social media. The voice of the creative and the voice of the invested move into a more public space than they occupied fifty years ago. The ability to move innovation quickly and engage in linkages is happening at a greater rate than ever before. Groupthink, crowd sourcing, and networks enable what was a single innovator to easily find counterparts throughout the system. The same is true for the invested and those who wish to keep change from happening. They too can find like-minded voices. This can create dark mobs of cynics who attempt to draw attention and focus away from the good work being undertaken by the new creatives.

Both the critics/cynics and the innovators can do terrible damage to one another and the mission of the church. Typically the cynics and critics launch attacks of snide remarks and make fun of and denigrate those who are struggling against all odds, fighting their way in the arena, innovating in the face of crises and dilemmas. The cynics' and critics' most powerful tool is shame. And they can whip up a shame storm quickly. This causes the innovators to put up their shields by fighting (taking the eye off the goal of dealing with the real issues), retreating (leaving the arena altogether by taking their gifts and talents out of the mix needed to solve the issues), or pleasing (dropping their work of creativity in order to try one day to sit in the cynics'/critics' seats).[4] So until the creative buzz rises above the din of deprivation, an organization can continue to spiral downward. This is exactly what is happening in our midst today.

None of this behavior is helpful, and in all cases our public arguing is detrimental to the mission. The innovators actually need that old disciplinary matrix to help them remember the narrative and understand the internal forces. The organization is always better off if it can stay together. And the organization needs the emerging disciplinary matrix of the innovators to continue to try new things. It is a kind of interdependent catholicity that adds pliability or anti-fragility into the church system. It is never a good thing for the community if individuals become detached or if you only have one group. Sometimes the isolation, criticism, and cynicism, despite sharing a desire to be loved, feel worthy of love, and connected to others, are so ugly that they actually push the new emerging community groups away from themselves.

I would also argue that, by dividing and becoming a church of only one kind of mission, one kind of liturgy, church, or this or that, we actually become more fragile. The reforming church divides and breaks apart until nothing much is left and its mission is defunct. A friend of mine used to say of her church, "We are a reforming reformed church reforming into nothing." The Anglican tradition of context-shaped mission is essential. In a world of multiple contexts, languages, culture, and people, it will require an Anglican breadth unseen in our previous history. Yet Anglicanism has this interdependent nature deep within its DNA and should be quite pliable, should its members choose to be.

I was an art student in college, and as a student, I received the gift of understanding the importance of helpful criticism from other artists who want me to succeed. Brené Brown is fond of telling me that we should listen carefully to critics who are deeply invested in our success and not so much to those who are not. In time I learned to let the critics' voices fall to the side if they were not invested in my success. This is good practice for anyone interested in amplifying the church through small batch church mission. Collaborate and cooperate with all those invested in the mission of the church, and let those comments from the cheap seats roll off your back.

As I look at our church, I see a wonderful and sacred mystery. I love it. I want it to grow and flourish. Sometimes I am in the cheap seats, and it is easy to be a critic and cynic. As a bishop, when I feel this tendency rise up in me, I remind myself that it is important to be quiet and let the innovators innovate. I can shut down creativity faster than anyone else. Ronald A. Heifetz, in *Leadership without Easy Answers*, a Harvard Business School publication, reminds leaders that one of the most important roles is giving cover to healthy voices of change.[5] I also know, if I don't think it is great or the best idea ever or if I have concerns about it failing, all I have to do is nix it. Good leaders know the importance of this power and use it sparingly. Why? If they are true leaders, they know a half-thought-out, good, or risky idea never has the potential for success if they shut them all down. New paradigms, reformations, revolutions, and life itself need space and an opportunity to take root.

Furthermore, sometimes ideas and creativity may fail on their first try but generate creativity within the system. This generative quality cannot be underestimated. Learning from mistakes or poor execution of a creative idea is always better for the organization than never attempting anything new. Such experimentation and attempts to try new things multiply and amplify the creative energy in the organization and make the organization stronger.

What is amazing in the current atmosphere in denominational churches across the country is the way in which cynicism and criticism are being used by those in power to shut down the very creativity the church needs to grow and thrive in the future. When both sides spend time sabotaging one another, the work of the gospel is not getting done.

We know the paradigm, the disciplinary matrix, is in fact shifting because we see and hear the harsh, mean-spirited, snarky, and disparaging words that the cynics and critics offer those who are trying new worship, experimenting with things like Ashes to Go, launching a pub mass, opening a coin-operated laundry ministry, attempting to offer a vision for a new church structure, creating different forms of Christian community, attempting different ways of engaging people, bringing about a new evangelical spirit of hope, and offering all manner of creativity. The list is a long one. Over six years of ministry as bishop, I have heard the voices, and I also see the potential and birthing of a new missionary age.

As the new paradigm is emerging, as innovation is taking root and as we try new things and old things pass away, the voices are getting louder. In some corners they are getting very loud indeed. And for those who have tried hard, worked in the arena all day, and had very real spiritual experiences, those disparaging words from people who stand outside the arena and just throw rotten tomatoes into it—via words, e-mails, Facebook statuses, and Twitter posts—sting.

The truth also is that sometimes I am the loudest voice speaking to myself, criticizing myself and offering voices of cynicism into the arena. I am tempted to take the critic's chair. When this happens and my voice is loud in my heart, incentivizing me to stop, be quiet, or leave the arena, I have to pause. "Listen for the creator's voice, or the harvest Lord's voice, listen for God as the gardener voice and hear God say, 'Fling out the seeds, put your shoulder to the Gospel plow, tend my garden, the harvest is plentiful, you are my laborer.'"

In that moment when I hear my Savior calling, I tell myself, "I know. I know the voices, and I can empathize with the critic's fear, yet we must together be courageous and let innovation happen." I am powerless to take away that sting that comes with creative work, especially good creative work. And when this happens, I like to read a few things that encourage me:

- "Here's to the crazy ones. The misfits. The rebels. The troublemakers. The round pegs in the square holes. The ones who see things differently. They're not fond of rules. And they have no respect for the status quo. You can quote them, disagree with them, glorify or vilify them. About the only thing you can't do is ignore them. Because they change things. They push the human race forward. And while some may see them as the crazy ones, we see genius. Because the people who are crazy enough to think they can change the world, are the ones who do" (Apple Computers advertisement).
- It is not the critic who counts; not the man who points out how the strong man stumbles, or where the doer of deeds could have done them better. The credit belongs to the man who is actually in the arena, whose face is marred by dust and sweat and blood; who strives valiantly; who errs, who comes short again and again, because there is no effort without error and shortcoming; but who does actually strive to do the deeds; who knows great enthusiasms, the great devotions; who spends himself in a worthy cause; who at the best knows in the end the triumph of high achievement, and

who at the worst, if he fails, at least fails while daring greatly, so that his place shall never be with those cold and timid souls who neither know victory nor defeat" (Teddy Roosevelt).
- "Do not be conformed to this world, but be transformed by the renewal of your mind, that by testing you may discern what is the will of God, what is good and acceptable and perfect" (Rom. 12:2).
- "For God so loved the world, that he gave his only Son, that whoever believes in him should not perish but have eternal life. For God did not send his Son into the world to condemn the world, but in order that the world might be saved through him" (John 3:16–17).
- "But let each one test his own work, and then his reason to boast will be in himself alone and not in his neighbor" (Gal. 6:4).
- "O, do not pray for easy lives. Pray to be stronger men! Do not pray for tasks equal to your powers. Pray for powers equal to your tasks! Then the doing of your work shall be no miracle. But you shall be a miracle. Every day you shall wonder at yourself, at the richness of life which has come to you by the grace of God" (Phillips Brooks, *Going Up to Jerusalem*)[6].

I dream of a church where we might support one another, as we say we are supposed to do. I dream of a church in which we might engage in real conversations instead of firing shrapnel into the air, hoping to hit something or someone. I dream of a church in which we might not feel less than for trying our best in the face of the critic.

I dream of a church that is no longer afraid of the revolution that has begun, one that understands we will need every possible kind of church, worship style, and creative evangelism to help us live into our future. I dream of a church that is filled with people less likely to criticize and more people willing to roll up their sleeves and find solutions to our mission challenges.

I dream of a church that is known as a sending church, a multiplying church, more than an attractional church. I dream of a church that multiplies and amplifies itself regardless of context. I dream of a church that is engaged in and investing in small batch communities that are local, organic, and sustainable.

I am mindful of all the critics' voices out there who are telling my brother and sister innovators that they are wrong, they are weakening the church, they are not serious/spiritual/theologically correct enough, and/or they aren't faithful enough. I raise a toast to you, your creativity, and your persistence for the hope of the future church in the face of the critic.

For in what you are trying to do, I see that wonderful and sacred mystery we call church. In you and your work, I see the Holy Spirit that brought all things into being. I see in you partners worth entering the arena with, and I see partners who will stay in the arena with hands joined.

In my books, *Church* and *A Generous Community*, I propose that a new understanding about the models, economies, and nature of Christian communities must change as we enter the new missionary age. They must become local, organic, and sustainable.[7] In order for our new communities to be successful, we must be locally focused. We must understand and meet our context with an open heart and listening ears.

In this attention to context, we are organic. We leave behind the binding structures of the inherited church of a bygone era and take with us a DNA of contextual Anglicanism that allows the Eucharist and reading of scripture to emerge in conversation with the community, becoming an organically grown Episcopal expression. By leaving behind structure and building up an organic community, we are able to have a much more sustainable mission expansion model. We are able to use free, shared, and public space, bringing down cost. A different vision of what is required for community returns to the gospel, Eucharist, and baptism and not what can be a burdensome overhead.

This is true for all denominations and the Episcopal Church. This book is about those models with a particular focus on the new small batch communities. I would like to shape our conversation around the nature of attractional models and sending/multiplying models of community. I want to ponder how they fit in a system. And I want to inspire you, the reader, to become a member of the missional community movement setting out from the Episcopal Church or your own denominational church.

So this book is my toast to you, my attempt to create a bit of safe space for you to run and play in and to join with you in dreaming of that which is even now taking root in our midst, small batch communities.

Dispatches from the Front: St. Lydia's Dinner Church

The Reverend Emily Scott, an ELCA pastor, is the founder of St. Lydia's Dinner Church. You can make your online pilgrim journey to St. Lydia's at www.stlydias.org. St. Lydia's is what I would call a missional community. Sponsored by a variety of co-founders, it created its own economy and mission plan focused on building a fresh community oriented around table fellowship. *This is their story.*

They gather every Sunday and Monday night to share a sacred meal, which they cook and eat together. Worship takes place around the table as they share food and conversation, as well as singing, prayers, and the study of scripture. The community hopes to reconnect neighbors, dispel isolation, and subvert the status quo, all around the kitchen table. Since moving into their own space (a storefront) in 2014, they have launched a co-working space where freelancers or those who would normally work from home work at St. Lydia's. We call it a "spiritually focused" workplace, where connections are made again around the table.

How It Began

The idea for St. Lydia's sparked after Emily Scott moved to New York and discovered that the folks she was meeting were spiritually hungry. They were looking for a place to be connected to one another in a city that can be isolating, overwhelming, and anonymous. Because apartments are small in New York and kitchens almost nonexistent (where the kitchen table is the first thing to go in a cramped apartment shared by roommates), the idea of coming together around a meal, just as the first followers of Jesus did, was immediately appealing and powerful. Their community started in the living room of a friend and quickly moved to a small Lutheran congregation in the East Village called Trinity Lower East Side, who made it possible for them to launch.

What They Learned

They have learned to trust (or to try to trust) that God is pulling together the threads and scraps of our lives into a patchwork that is surprising and unexpected long before they ever expect that God is at work. That communities are like organisms. They need time to breathe, grow, and rest. They learned that vision and implementation are very different but must be closely aligned and the Holy Spirit is extremely mischievous.

What They Might Do Differently

The biggest thing that Emily and her leadership are trying to learn is how to effectively share the work of ministry and empower the congregants of the church to lead and follow their own call. This means not only getting out of the way, but also creating structures that allow people to participate and feel like their voice is heard. While Emily is responsible for holding out the vision and the focus of the community and keeping everyone headed toward that vision, she recognizes that she can also be constantly giving it away to lay leaders who are ready to take the vision and run with it.[8]

Questions:

1. What does the phrase "paradigm shift" mean to you? Do you think the church finds herself amidst a paradigm shift? Why or why not?
2. Do you see yourself more as a keeper of the old paradigm or as a new, emerging innovator? How might both roles be important in the future church?
3. What might a local, organic, and sustainable Christian community look like? Can you envision being part of such a community? Have you ever experienced such a community?
4. What does the word *affection* mean to you? How does affection grow in a Christian community?

Recommendations for Further Reading

Art of the Start by Guy Kawasaki

Yours for the Asking by Reynold Levy

Ten Most Common Mistakes Made by New Church Starts by James Griffith and William Easum

Chapter 2

From Opaque History to Autopoetic Mission

Nassim Taleb, in his book *Black Swan*, writes that we misobserve reality and history because we can't observe everything. And so we make up stuff, including patterns.[9] This is, in part, why it has been so difficult to deal with the current examination of church attendance. Too many things are involved in the situation; therefore, no single pattern of observation or solution will solve what is an organic, interconnected web of relationships that stretch through our congregations and out into the wider culture.

Economist Daniel Kahneman agrees with Taleb, and I am afraid it adds even more suspicion to the way in which we tell our stories about congregational church history. He writes, "The confidence that individuals have in their beliefs depends mostly on the quality of the story they can tell about what they see, even if they see little."[10] This is a principle he calls "WYSIATI," or "what you see is all there is."[11] Kahneman says the systematic part of our brains is lazy, so we typically jump to conclusions based upon intuitive impressions rather than difficult thinking.[12] You can believe this is not true, but the Nobel prize-winning economist has four hundred pages of in-depth research that says your bias about his opinion is based upon intuition and not reality.

In the wake of this reading, I have begun to wonder about how we interpret our own history as a church and congregations. I have begun to think a bit differently about the church history that I inherited or thought I saw. I probably should say it made me rethink how I had ordered my own leadership within the intuition based upon the church history I learned. As

I reflected on my own biases, I was amazed at what I discovered. Church history is taught in a linear fashion, and because you can only see what you are taught (and WYSIATI), it is no wonder that we have developed an oversimplified understanding of our church, its origins, and its perfect trajectory to this moment in time.

The defense of new prayer books and liturgical movements has amplified the notion of a linear church history. Such a history goes something like this. We have always been heading in this direction, so we have naturally arrived here, doing exactly what was always required. The predictable success has been ours. In fact, if you are not having success, you are simply not working hard enough or doing the right things. This way of thinking denies any external force that may be operating within the context of the past, present, or future.

Of course, according to Taleb's and Kahneman's suspicions about observation and history, this is crazy thinking. It is actually called a "hindsight bias." Again Kahneman writes, "The mind that makes up narratives about the past is a sense-making organ ... A general limitation of the human mind is its imperfect ability to reconstruct past states of knowledge, or beliefs that have changed."[13] If we are going to ponder what the future may look like, we have to come to terms with the fact that the past probably was not much like what our intuitive biases tell us it was like.

Let us look again, as if for the first time, at the formation of the earliest Christian communities or what we call church. Why? They don't look anything like what we think of as church life, congregational life, today.

The earliest texts seem to reveal that the first followers of Jesus lived in a variety of communities. They lived in urban and rural areas. Many of the first followers of Jesus were Jews, and plenty of others were not. A lot of different people were reacting to the teachings of Jesus and other reform movements. This intermingling of diverse people on diverse social levels, each living out his or her faith, created an environment of energized innovation and creativity. This is certainly a vision of the early followers that is recorded and remarked upon in the Gospels, the book of Acts, and the Epistles. Only our sense-making mind pretends to see one pattern in these diverse texts. From the very beginning, the Christian movement was a broad movement, a catholic movement.

I think we can also say that the Jesus movement was, in its earlier days, a kind of subculture within the culture and went unnoticed for quite a while. Yet the Jesus movement grew in every social context with a multiplicity of incarnations. It was not like Jesus was resurrected, the Holy Spirit came down, and boom! There were churches with an average Sunday attendance (ASA) of 250.

The letters of Paul to the different communities offer an early and clear record that one way individuals got together was in their own homes. Paul is continually remarking on "so-and-so's house." Paul's letters are often addressed to a church, but it is also true, within each city church, let's say Corinth, for instance, there were a number of small house churches. In Paul's letter to Philemon, it is clear that his house church was one of many in the city of Colossa.[14] These most likely involved a variety of individuals with different faith experiences and connections to the home where the group met.[15] We must dismiss any theory that says there were only house churches or there were only urban churches. We see clearly in the texts that both coexisted. In fact there were other kinds of communal response to Jesus and his resurrection that coexisted also.

Early followers of Jesus were transforming and creating clubs, guilds, and associations. There were colleague groups and burial societies.[16] These were organized a bit differently than the house communities and the larger city clusters. There seems to be a patron client relationship whereby individuals participated in the societies and supported them through their donations and presence. (This is not unlike some of the groups we see forming today in the research called *How We Gather*.) These were more exclusive groups with particular liturgies and criteria for belonging than the house church.

At the same time, while the Pauline churches appear to have been more unified in terms of social rank, the societies, oddly enough, were more open to a cross-section of people because they were based less on the same family of origin or part of the community and more on the criteria of belonging.[17] These societies coexisted as self-contained and unique organizations. They were particularly located within their context.[18]

There was, in fact, still another type of community that was randomly being generated during the same period of time. Many of the first followers of Jesus were Jews, so they founded communities within synagogues. Many of these groups would soon be identified as Christian and would be kicked out of the synagogues. So the nature and liturgy of synagogue worship was very important to this unique community. In time and throughout the Mediterranean region, unused or abandoned synagogues would be reinhabited or taken over by Christians. So some of the first buildings we might call churches began their lives as synagogues. The ones we know from Paul's letters and archeological digs are Duro Europos, Stobi, and Delos.[19]

Schools were still another kind of Christian community. Similar to philosophical schools of the day, this is where followers of Jesus would gather around a particular teacher or noted leader. The disciples met and learned together and debated one another.[20] These learning groups might include professionals or students. Discourse and guidance given to the disciples were part of the unique nature of these groups. They grew, and some would become communities in and of themselves.[21]

While the cities appeared to be swelling with a variety of communities, so too were rural areas. Some of these forms existed in the smaller rural areas. Yet out of the desert came a more communal expression of early Christianity. Sects, special groups, and movements of God fearers had been part of Middle Eastern life for centuries before the time of Jesus. After Jesus's resurrection, there emerged parallel communities of cave-dwelling desert fathers, small groups of praying women, and communes filled with people who believed in separating themselves out of the society in order to prepare for Jesus's return. These movements can easily be seen as the seeds of the monastic movements to come.

During the fastest-growing time of church history, we can see that multiple groups of Christians were gathering together in a variety of forms. They were small batch communities characterized by their local nature. They grew out of organic relationships. And they were sustainable because they used existing structures, homes, or ones with no structure.

I have mentioned the ones we know about. Think about that for a moment. We know about these types of communities. But this cannot possibly be a complete inventory of the Christian community types that existed. There were, in fact, many kinds. Remember WYSIWTI. These are only the ones we have read about or dug up. There were, in fact, many forms and ways of participating. People believed different things and worshipped in various ways. People gathered at different times of the week in different places. There was a universality, a broadness to their life that actually resulted in the expansion of Christian community. So what happened?

In this diverse, living, growing, thriving period of our communal life, the focus was upon relationships. The relationship with the risen Lord and their relationships with one another mattered most. Space, liturgy, vessels, roles, theologies, unanimity, and even definitive ways of being community were varied. They were also all secondary or tertiary concerns. The vessels and the spaces were not defining concerns of the community. Archeological evidence reveals that commonplace objects, places, and meals were the primary locus of the relational act of gathering. We can imagine full participation in the goings-on of these familial gatherings. There was a give-and-take, and roles were most likely shared. In the few formal societies, the roles were more defined.

As the communities (the ones we know about) grew and organized, more emphasis moved to the defining roles of place and liturgy. By 300 AD, we have unified and common liturgies, a developing customary,[22] and vessels made specifically for liturgical use.[23] The spaces begin to be organized around the gathering of the people, as opposed to early space, which just happened to be where people found themselves and where they organized themselves. The importance of space and content would continue to evolve.

By the eighth century, the ordinary has become the special. The ordinary household materials gathered and used for the breaking of common bread in whatever place the faithful gathered are now transformed. The pottery cup and plate taken from the cupboard now are gold and silver formed for the special purpose of the Lord's Supper. Along with the special vessels comes the standardization of the service itself.[24] Special buildings set apart from the common home now become community centers for the life of the faithful. Abbeys for those who follow the strictest of rules have now formed. Shrines dot the Holy Land. People make pilgrimages to see the sacred sites, reenacting the moments of Christ's life. There seems to be a never-ending evolution of growth in hierarchy, the setting aside of places of worship, and the formalization of worship. Even what were normal street clothes in the first century are now beautiful vestments signifying roles and work in the Eucharistic feast.

By 1517, buildings and liturgy are no longer about the people but about the action. This is the high-water mark of the universal faith that is Christianity. People no longer are participants in the way they were in the early days. The liturgy is no longer for the hearing or the responding. People are distant, and what is happening is mysterious and not very earthly. While we can imagine that there were hosts in some early communities, we know for sure that many were simply householders. By the sixteenth century, we have a high priesthood that is in charge of the holy items.[25] The holy world is wholly separate from the real world, and the heavenly banquet table is carefully and ritually prepared by the professional.

Now we have arrived at the Reformation. The great divide is also the great moment of reinvention of the church. As the world itself and culture were focused upon the nature of knowing—epistemology—the reinvention was all about understanding. The great movements of the Reformation were about the Bible, liturgy, and language. There was a rediscovery of a living theology. All of this was broadcast in the language of the people. Homes and churches were filled with a new vibrancy of faith.

This, of course, cannot be understated. The reform would eventually spread, and Christianity would continue to grow. But it grew within the vessel that had become the norm, a church building. The church is the building where the people go for the sacraments (Roman) or to hear the living word preached (reformed). What happens during the succeeding three hundred years is a bumpy road but mostly unchanged until the invention of free time.

While some will want to focus on the monastic reformations or the discoveries of ancient manuscripts or liturgical revivals, I want to focus on the creation of free time. The Victorians are responsible for this invention. No matter what we look at, the creation of public parks, the decrease of the workweek, the increase in what people called pastime, the invention of baseball as the best way to spend that pastime, or the growing understanding of something called "childhood," all came into fashion during the nineteenth century.[26]

During the Industrial Revolution, Victorians were the first to begin to think differently about time that was not spent working. Think about it for just a moment. Prior to the Victorian age, people worked all the time. It was survival that set the hours of the day. From sunup to sundown, people worked every day of the week. They would only occasionally make their way to the local shrine for the holy feast day of their town. But now there is time. What began to happen next will tell the tale for a hundred years. The church began to grow in attendance. Not only did the Victorians invent pastime, they decided to spend it going to church. The minister and preaching were some of the best entertainment there was to be had.

The expansion of cities, growth in population in the West, and the unchallenged sacred time of Wednesday nights and Sunday mornings saw the great expansion—explosion—in church attendance. Yay for free time! This was to become a moment in our church history not unlike the very high Middle Ages when we were humming along. We had a great capacity, and the church expanded. By the end of this boom in the 1950s, the diocese I serve had planted five congregations a year for a decade. It almost doubled what we had had for the previous century. The Diocese of Texas was not alone in this expansion. Resources of the empire-rich Western church began to build monolithic bureaucracies and hierarchies. In our own tradition, our presiding bishop appeared on the cover of *Time* magazine! Money-rich, we sent out missionaries, and our church itself began to expand into new countries, completing the global vision of the nineteenth-century mission movements.

We also turned inward. New scholarship allowed for a reinvention of liturgy in our tradition, though this was true for all the mainline denominations. By the twentieth century the liturgical movement had returned the central action of the Eucharist to weekly worship. The liturgical renewal movement also brought a new liturgical fundamentalism with it. We became overly focused on the words we say, the words the priest says, and the words of the Bible. Fundamentalism sneaked in, and Christians began to argue over inherency. Politics crept in, and we began to argue about cultural issues. Words and their meaning became important, and we argued over the gender of God, sexuality, the gender of ministers, and divorced people. We argued, and we argued. Along with the rest of the Western culture, we divided ourselves into camps at war with one another. We began to break apart our churches, as if playing out C. S. Lewis' *The Screwtape Letters*, in which a senior devil instructs the disciple to keep the Christians fighting amongst themselves so the mission will never happen. Saint Paul has similar warnings about division. Yet we become the arbiters of truth, and the great dismantling of Western Christianity begins.

I am not judging this part of our history, though it would have been nice if someone had been paying attention to the dramatic changes taking place. I think you can only see what you can see. The church and her leadership did not see what was coming. Here is the important thing: because we did not do evangelism and discipleship but waited for people to come through our doors, today we are in trouble and out of shape.

At the same moment that we were busy, there was a seismic shift in the culture. Philosopher Charles Taylor, in his book *A Secular Age*, called it a "mass phenomenon."[27] The culture, Taylor offers, is caught in an immanent frame. The mechanical world jettisoned a "hierarchy of being," and there was an "atrophy of a sense of God."[28] The transcendent world was rejected for a natural world without mystery. Everything could be explained in reference to itself. There was no need for the individual life to be dependent upon or in relationship with God.

Instead the "buffered human being" was self-sufficient.[29] Even society was able to reveal its own "blueprint" for how things are to "hang together" for the "mutual benefit" of the whole.[30] In the end there would be no need for God or religion. The church was, all in all, unprepared to speak a living word into this culture shift. In fact the church willingly adapted to it and settled into a diaspora relationship with the culture.

Harvey Cox wrote in his musing on the secular city, "The failure of modern theology is that it continues to supply plausible answers to questions that fewer and fewer people are asking."[31] Not unlike the twentieth century, we continue to answer questions and problems from a period that no longer exists.

Moreover these are just a few themes and trajectories that we can see. Our whole history is an intermingling of diverse webs tied into individual personalities, stories, and cultural shifts. A whole industry of PhD dissertations has evolved around tracing the infinite connections across this past horizon of history, revealing the myriad connections and linkages throughout any one culture and the church.

autopoiesis — self producing [handwritten annotation]

What the present church has inherited as the view of ourselves and how we are to proceed from this point forward is flawed. In the end we can only see and know in part what God is doing. We must let go of a number of things in order to frame our future conversation. We must hold the following lightly: our categories, measurements for success, narrow leadership job descriptions, and economic models for doing church. In other words, we must let go of the core belief that this is the way it has been and this is the way it will be. And if we just work harder using the same the model, everything will return to normal, like in the 1950s.

I am not the only one challenging the old model. The emerging church movement is challenging what church looks like on the surface. They are trying to make church better and accessible to people outside the church. While creative, it is still wrestling within the straitjacket of the current church model. A lot of consultants have even made a career out of telling the boxed church, if they will just mimic what the emerging church folks have to say, they will be okay and reach those millennials out there. My friend, The Reverend Paul Fromberg, says, "The emerging Church is like a new toy, the church will soon break it." Still another group of consultants has spent a lot of time sharing what the megachurches have learned, wooing the struggling masses to imitate concepts that themselves are locked into particularities.

As we say in the South, all our efforts are like putting lipstick on a pig. Until we break open the box and let out the living church, we are stuck. Imagine what would happen if we really freed our leaders who are interested in small batch church to set up shop outside. Diocesan leadership has to be willing to let these creative leaders be unshackled from their standards of measurement to create new mission criteria. Author Margaret Wheatley writes,

> Life is about creation. This ability of life to create itself is captured in a strange-sounding new word, *autopoiesis* (from Greek, meaning self-production or self-making). Autopoiesis is life's fundamental process for creating and renewing itself, for growth and change. A living system is a network of processes in which every process contributes to all the other processes. The entire network is engaged together in producing itself.[32]

We must see differently with new eyes and work differently with new ideas if we are to allow for a living, thriving autopoietic church.

One of my favorite books is Simon Winchester's *The Map That Changed the World: William Smith and the Birth of Modern Geology*. It is about the story of William Smith (1769–18369), a geologist and surveyor unofficially known as the father of geology in England. What he did was essentially measure England and Wales. He figured out, not only could he map the earth and where things are, he also figured you could map the strata of rocks beneath the surface. His work altered completely how we view the world around us and beneath our feet. This was important because it changed our perspective.

Do you remember when you first looked at Google Earth? It was amazing. Brian McClendon, a Google executive, wrote in a blog post that they were engaging in the "never-ending quest for the perfect map."[33] He wrote, "We've been building a comprehensive base map of the entire globe—based on public and commercial data, imagery from every level (satellite, aerial and street level) and the collective knowledge of our millions of users."[34]

Jerry Brotton, professor of Renaissance studies at Queen Mary University, London, commented, "All cultures have always believed that the map they valorize is real and true and objective and transparent."[35] He continued, "All maps are always subjective ... Even today's online geospatial applications on all your mobile devices and tablets, be they produced by Google or Apple or whoever, are still to some extent subjective maps."[36]

Uri Friedman reflects in an article in *The Atlantic*, "12 Maps That Changed the World," "There are ... no perfect maps—just maps that (more-or-less) perfectly capture our understanding of the world at discrete moments in time."[37]

It is thus clear that our perspective also affects our movement out into the world. Our perspective affects the manner in which we navigate our context. The complexity of our mission will require us not only to have the prophetic vision of our core mission but also the means by which to achieve it. Not unlike a cartographer, we will need to use some of what we have learned in the past to help us navigate, interpret, and engage with the new world that is evolving outside our church doors.

The church must be a place with a perspective outside its walls with a developing map that will change our world. We are invited by Christ and the Holy Spirit to leave the building (like Elvis) and go out into the real world with the living, risen Lord who is even now in the community already and at work there. The church in the midst of the city of the living God will have to be gentle and meek as it steps out of the shadow of its shrine to a church that does not exist any longer. The church will have to mourn with all sorts and conditions of people. The church will have to proclaim in word the commandments of our God: to love our neighbor as Jesus loved us. The church will have to show mercy as Jesus shows mercy. And the church will have to seek a nonviolent immersion with the world outside its walls, no matter how persecuted it may be. We must be fearless in taking our place in the public square, throwing aside the notion that religion and faith are private matters. Through invitation, partnership, and participation, we must remap the streets, public places, and spaces as venues for liturgy and life of the church beyond our walls.

It is true, for some, the city may always be a symbol of evil, corruption, and decay. But for the living church, the city is a symbol of life, human cooperation, human potential, the ever-expanding family of God, and corporate salvation. Our cities are cities of the living God. Only autopoietic missionary Christian communities will survive. Our map will not be perfect, but it will give us a new perspective of where we are in the new mission context.

Stepping out, looking around, and figuring out where we really stand, I believe the most effective missionary and mission organization will be those that are team-led. They will be diverse ethnically, embracing the multiple languages and cultures we find outside our churches. Successful mission will be dependent upon blended leadership talent, ages, and communication styles. Most importantly, though, is that, wherever the individual moves and sets up a tent of meeting for ministry, there will have to be investment in the local community. We believe, as Margaret Wheatley says, "Relationships are not just interesting ... they are all there is to reality."[38] This will mean, just as the world around us is organically connected, so too our organization will have to be organic and rich with networks that connect us throughout the world around us. We are going to have to let go and return to a very rich and diverse understanding of community life and growth.

C. S. Lewis speaks of love as the binding principle to community. The Reverend Dr. Scott Bader-Saye, professor of ethics and dean of faculty at Seminary of the Southwest, in a presentation on affection, connected Paul's teaching with that of C. S. Lewis. C. S. Lewis talks about the quality of this love and connectedness in his book *The Four Loves*.[39] He writes that the bonds of affection that we have for one another are essential in connecting us to God. We can have agape love, but it is limited because it can only be one directional.[40] Love connected to God, as in Jesus's and Paul's teaching, is mutual. It flows among all those involved. We might have friendship as one of the loves, but most often friendship is something shared among those who are most like us.[41]

This has been shown to be true in the most recent Pew Research poll on the politicization of America. It finds, not only are like-minded people likely to live in the same places and like the same things, they are also more likely to hang out with friends who believe similar things.[42] This means that friendship can easily lead to isolating communities. The mission of the gospel is for the Christian community to be open to everyone.

The third love is Eros, and this is intimate love and even more exclusive.[43] Affection, Lewis offers, is the broadest kind of love. It is the kind that Paul encourages all followers of Jesus to have. It is the kind of love that is the most natural and is required in all the others. Bader-Saye believes, in affection, we have the broadest ability to love.[44] He writes we have the ability for mutuality and it is not dependent upon friendship, infatuation, or attraction.[45] He says that affection makes possible all the rest.[46] "Affection is connection," writes American author and economist Wendell Berry.[47] Affection is the quality of relationship that Jesus speaks about and the quality of relationships that people are seeking as they yearn in the midst of a disjointed and disconnected world.

What is true theologically and spiritually is true technologically. Today people place a high value on connecting to their peers, resources, entertainment, and finances; therefore, relationship communities that are Christian will place high importance on the work of connection. The future church will be marked by affection above all else.

I have learned from the "maker movement," a secular term used to describe the new small batch industrial age, that it takes the same amount of energy and time to customize as it does to mass-produce items. We are seeing a rise in personal fabrication that then is marketed and connected to friends and neighbors. We are in the midst of what is called a "small batch movement."

The small batch bourbon, beer, and bakery movements are good examples of how innovators are connecting to their peers. Scale is no longer the quintessential goal of business. More and more people are baking, distilling, and creating businesses in their homes and selling to their friends. What is coming into view is a society, and that is restructuring itself organically. This is our mission field.

Bob Johansen writes, "In fields as diverse as education, governance, science, and health, amplified individuals are boldly engaged in de-institutionalizing production, taking value out of traditional ways of organizing, and actively building alternative platforms and tools."[48]

Children are writing computer programs, creating art, and building their own networks. Adults are crafting things in their garages. Technology and communication tools are shifting monthly. New micro-economy and secondary markets are growing. New currencies and new forms of connecting with investors are changing start-ups with crowd-sourced technology. Science projects and experiments run twenty-four hours a day using people across the globe. Many are volunteers. People are relating and co-creating at a colossal level.

Johansen comments on this by saying, "The future lies in micro-contributions by large networks of people creating value on a scale previously unthinkable, bringing sociality and social connectivity back into our economic transactions, in the process redefining notions of rewards, incentives, growth, and currencies."[49]

This will affect how our Christian communities work and build relationships. This means that Christian communities, thanks to technology and the maker movement, can exist on limited small budgets with few staff and still reach large numbers of people through their ministry.[50] The hallmark of the Christian community of the future is that they will connect people and, most of all, connect people to God.

In order to discover our new context, we need to look at the world around us and imagine how the current living city offers a vision of an autopoietic church. We can see now the artifacts for our future.

Dispatches from the Front: Laundry Love

Scott Claasen and Kevin Lake, along with Jimmy Bartz are the founders of Laundry Love, a Greenfield community of Thad's Place in Santa Monica, California. You can make your online pilgrim journey to Laundry Love on the web here, http://thads.org/events/thads-laundry-love-venice-monday-930. *This is their story.*

On the last Monday evening of every month, a group of volunteers from Thad's takes over a Laundromat in Venice Beach where they, along with the locals, make community. For the next several hours, they provide quarters, detergent, and other basic supplies to people who have gathered to have their clothes cleaned. The majority of the people who come are homeless or transitionally housed.

They call it Laundry Love. They like to say they are doing laundry with an emphasis on love. Their primary goal is not necessarily to do laundry, but to be present and loving to whomever they meet. That said, they do a lot of laundry. They tend to wash upward to five hundred loads of laundry in the course of one night.

One of the miraculous things about this simple community is the way in which people come together. They think of Laundry Love as the modern-day foot washing. There is something about washing clothes that brings out the vulnerability in both the guests and those who serve. Perhaps it is the intimacy of handling clothes. Maybe it is the amount of free time between the beginning and end of the machine cycles. Or maybe it is simply the opportunity to stand face-to-face with someone who is both very different from you and very much the same. In any case, everybody wins. Love wins.

How It Began

Laundry Love Venice Beach is a direct descendent of Laundry Love Huntington Beach. For a few years, good friends of Thad's, Christian Kassoff and Stephen Bruce, had been interested in starting something like a Thad's. They called it Thom's. Their hope was that Thom's could be oriented around service in some unique way. They heard about a Laundry Love program in Santa Ana. They visited and loved it. It turns out that Laundry Love had started years before in Ventura. Slowly but surely, it was spreading around the country. In early July 2013, the Thad's community volunteered at Laundry Love Huntington Beach. Two months later, they had their own Laundry Love in Venice Beach.

It is noteworthy that Laundry Love was and is a largely lay-led activity. Although The Reverend Jimmy Bartz gave the motivating spark, Kevin Lake and Scott Claassen, ordained now but not when we started, did most of the work of developing the community, doing outreach, and running the groups of washers. This is important because visiting clergy mention that they fear they do not have the energy or time to take on another activity. Laundry Love is absolutely something that can be done with minimal requirements from clergy. Of course they encourage clergy to participate, as it is a life-giving, eye-opening, heart-molding experience that invariably leaves you filled with divine love and grace.

What They Learned

1. They learned what size washing machine can take a sleeping bag and what size cannot.
2. They learned where people sleep on the street in their town.
3. They learned that knowing homeless people enriches their daily life and teaches them a whole lot about knowing Jesus.
4. They learned that some businesses do not like homeless people, even if they pretend otherwise.
5. They learned that you can do the same amount of laundry and spread the same amount of love in a big, beautiful Laundromat as you can in a dingy, small one.
6. They learned the value of a bathroom.
7. They learned the value of clean clothes.

8. They learned it might be more helpful to provide one service and do it well.

In other words, it's better in Venice Beach to do laundry than doing laundry, giving out pizza, and providing other services. You might say it's okay if the community is created simply around doing laundry. Furthermore:

1. They learned how to handle a chainsaw.
2. They learned how to listen and love someone who is neither sober nor sane.
3. They learned how heavy a night's worth of quarters is.
4. They learned their particular group of homeless folks love to send Christmas cards if given the opportunity.
5. They learned that some people will take advantage of anything.
6. They learned they didn't know very much.
7. They learned how nice it was to come home, take a shower, and get into bed exhausted.

What They Might Do Differently

From the very beginning, they would do everything possible to have a good relationship with the neighbors, the landowner, the business owner, and other interested parties. That said, it's not easy to get all of those people to agree.

While it is not something they would do differently, they do think that Laundry Love needs constant revision and adaptation to the needs of the community that develops. Before starting a Laundry Love, any group needs to assess the transportation options, other services, and general sentiment of the population they hope to serve. In other words, they would hope that Laundry Love Venice Beach continues to evolve to better serve the needs of the community at the time.[51]

Questions

1. Bishop Doyle suggests that our linear telling of church history fails to do justice to the complexity and variety of Christian community that existed in the early church. Do you agree? How might rethinking church history change our modern understanding of Christian community?

2. Do you believe that people today enjoy a lot of free time? Why or why not? How might an answer to that question impact our theology of mission?
3. Bishop Doyle says, in the future, "the most effective missionary organizations will be those that are team-led." Do you agree? Why or why not?
4. Do you believe the church needs to rethink how we measure success? In the past, how has the church measured success? How should the church measure success in the future?

Recommendations for Further Reading

Start Something That Matters by Blake Mycoskie

Jesus and the Disinherited by Howard Thurman

The Gifts of Imperfection by Brené Brown

P. 27 - Create Christian Communities so people may come together & experience the grace of God creating a culture of shared grace to work & serve others & to play & celebrate life.

Chapter 3

Renewed Mission Field

Let us begin by looking at the urban environment. The church, for many years, has been focused overwhelmingly on the suburban environment for mission, at least since the suburban migration of the 1950s. We will address this in a few pages. We have ignored the signs that reveal that an urban mass migration is coming. No matter what your observation bias may be, we are in a massive global population shift into the world's cities. Today over half the world's population live in urban areas. Some estimates reveal, in many countries, the percentage is a lot higher. We are entering an urbanized world. We begin here in this chapter because this is the place where we have the most opportunity to see the future and move into it.

I believe, when we think about cities, we think about downtowns, office buildings, skyscrapers, and the like. We think about the infrastructure. This particular hiccup gets us into trouble because, as we think about the city, we think about the church in the city. And by church we mean the church building. A city is made up of people though. It has inhabitants. A report from the Institute for the Future reads, "For future smart cities to thrive, it must be centered around people, not just infrastructure."[52]

Dan Hill, CEO of Fabrica, a communications research center (http://www.fabrica.it), says, "We don't make cities in order to make buildings and infrastructure or, indeed, technology—that's a side effect of making cities. We create cities to come together, to create culture or commerce, to live, to work, to play—to create more people."[53] The problem with how we imagine our urban mission is the same problem many in the commercial world face. We forget it is about people and not the structures of church.

Purpose of Community

The discussion around smart cities might well echo our own. Anthony Townsend, Research Director at IFTF and author of the upcoming book *SMART CITIES: Big Data, Civic Hackers, and the Quest for a New Utopia*, writes,

> Citizens are not employees or customers, they have to be dealt with on a different basis. So the idea that you can install the smart city like an upgrade and expect people to just live with it—especially when it takes power away from them—means they're not going to accept it. So you have to engage with them and grow it from the bottom up.[54]

He continues,

> This is an age in which very big things can come from massively coordinated human activity that doesn't necessarily get planned from the top down. We need to stop thinking about building smart cities like a mainframe—which is this industry vision—and think about it more like we built the web, as loosely intercoupling networks.[55]

Dan Hill talks about these smart citizens,[56]

> Despite the heavy infrastructure-led visions of the systems integrators and IT corporations, the most interesting and productive use of contemporary technology in the city is here, literally in the hands of citizens, via phones and social media ... The dynamics of social media have been adopted and adapted in the last few years to enable engaged and active citizens to organize rapidly and effectively; a network with a cause. Smart citizens' seem to emerge at a far faster rate than we're seeing more formal technology-led smart cities emerging ... In the face of institutional collapse, active citizens are knitting together their own smart city, albeit not one envisaged by the systems integrators and technology corporations.[57]

What does this mean for us? We do not build communities to build church buildings. We do not do our diocesan work in order to maintain the infrastructure of church. We are in the business of creating Christian communities so people may come together and experience the grace of God, creating a culture of sharing grace to work and serve others and to play and celebrate life.

Just like many city planners and governments, we forget our work is about people. We have created a system by which people are here to support the church rather than the church support the people in making community. When we do this, we take power and energy out of the organization. We take life out of the organism. The only way to build a vital and healthy mission in the future will be to engage with people in real time where they are and to listen and work with them to create the new living church.

Consider the largest aspen grove in the world, the Pando Grove in Utah, and many think it is to be one of the largest living organisms in the world with a massive single underground root system. Likewise, our cities and our churches, if seen as giant organisms, can and will be part of "massively coordinated human activity."[58] The church, if it wishes to be present as a living organism within the life of the city, will have to couple with the vibrant city networks. It will be autopoietic, that is, porous. It will have to build commons—both electronic and human— throughout the city's mainframe. The church will have to participate in organizing, gathering, and ministering through the same media relationships that people use in their daily lives. We are looking at a world of smart citizens, and that will mean we are living in a world of smart community members.

When talking about the future of cities, there are lessons to be learned about what is happening now. Some city planners look at Hongdae in South Korea. It used to be a very traditional suburb. Urbanization occurred, and masses of people moved into the area. People built up the city by adding onto already existing structures. Office life, shopping, dining, and small businesses were built onto existing homes and buildings. They were not following the building code. Instead of stopping this massive DIY movement, the leaders of the city worked with the people. They changed some of their regulations and began to steer the life of the growing metropolitan area into a productive and healthy future.[59]

What changed? Leaders saw that the city itself was a platform interacting in relationship with the people. Most master plans make the people conform. This plan adapted to the people. City planners are asking themselves today: how can you open up your codes and make a platform that is open and can adapt to bottom-up practices?[60] The reality is that these same questions will lead to exciting discoveries in the urban, suburban, and rural environments if we will but invite them.

We still are in the business of planting churches and hoping people will come into them. We have a church development strategy that seeks to have the people conform to its existing model. The church has an opportunity to look out and see that we should be interacting with our people in the mission field. Our platform of structure and polity needs to adapt to the world and people around us and not the other way round. We are to be a people-led community with the organization/platform supporting the work. We are not to be an organization/platform that leads and is supported by people. This is a very important and integral cultural change. It is a necessary organizational flip.

How will we begin to be an organization willing to play with our people? How will we engage with them and follow them out into the world? We will have to deliver valuable, low-cost, lightweight, moveable, transferable, multi-use infrastructure to our people. This is what we can do with our organization's economy of scale. At the same time, we will have to allow our people to lead us. The church organization has to adapt to the people we intend to reach.

A Decentralized Model

A new model will be essential. In 1962 children were hiding under their desks in America, practicing for what seemed like a sure thing, a nuclear attack from the Soviet Union. By every indication nuclear proliferation was a likely reality.[61] The Cuban Missile Crisis was hot, and the USSR and the United States were engaged in massive nuclear buildups and ballistic missile systems. Both countries were trying to figure out how they might survive an attack and if they should, in fact, attack first.[62] Hawks on both sides of the world were sure they had the answer. I believe we probably are not fully aware of how close we came to an extinction event.

One of the issues for the United States was how would the leaders speak to one another, post-event? Because the military works on a command control network, they needed one that would survive the disaster.[63] Enter RAND Corporation. RAND was working with the military on a number of projects at the time. A researcher in their office, Paul Baran, who was involved in a lot of a fancy work that probably most people in the day would have believed was stolen from a spaceship in Area 51. Nevertheless the hardworking Baran slaved away at trying to figure out this problem. His solution, and therefore RAND's solution, for the United States was to build a "more robust communications network using 'redundancy' and 'digital' technology."[64] Of course nobody really believed that Baran's idea was possible, so they dismissed it, thus prolonging the creation of the World Wide Web by a decade or more.

Basically Baran's idea was that a centralized communication system relies on only one switch to communicate, store, and send out messages. A decentralized system would do the same but have several kinds of backup or other relays. Essentially both of these would easily fall victim to an attack, as one particular area might completely cut off a region where communication was needed or, worse, in the case of the destruction of the centralized system where the effect would completely shut down communication altogether. Baran imagined a different kind of system.

Figure 1. Baran's example of network nodes (Paul Baran, August 1964).

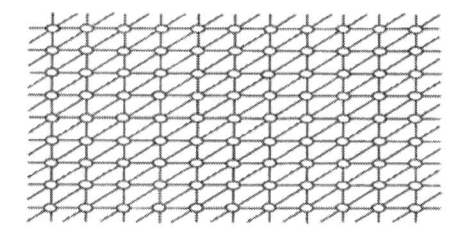

Basically Baran created a distributed system of communications. Through the system, information is carried from one node to another on its own. Each node, while still part of the unit, acts autonomously and independently. It receives the piece of information and then stores and sends it along to the next node. If there were a problem with one of the nodes, the information could take another route to its destination.[65] Here is what Baran actually offered in his paper:

Figure 2. Baran's application of his design to a real-world geometry and landscape (Baran, August 1964).

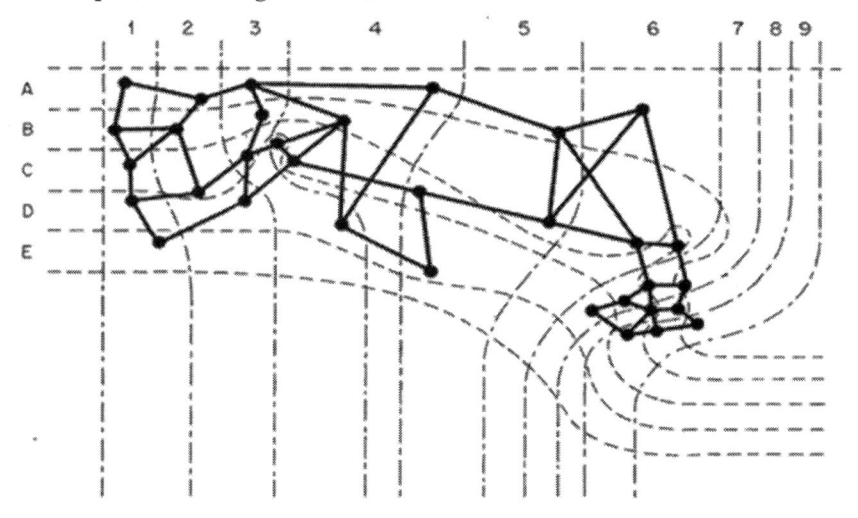

Figure 3. Illustration of a centralized, decentralized, and distributed network (Baran, August 1964).

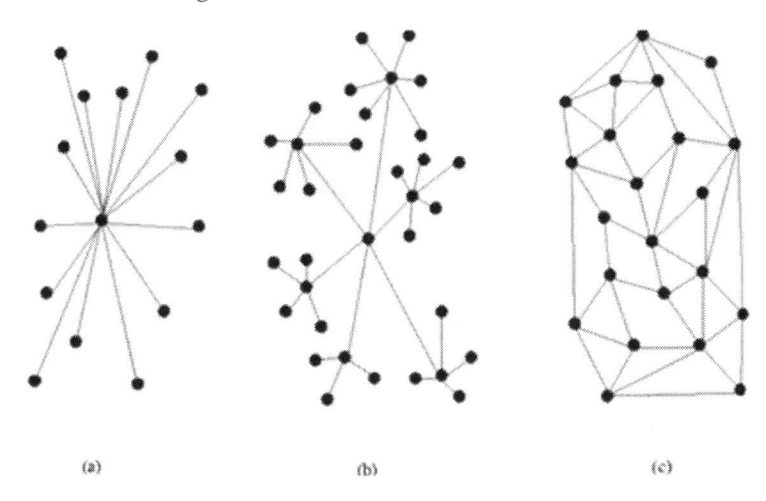

(a)   (b)   (c)

Wired magazine interviewed Baran in 2003, and he talked about the system he had created,

> Around December 1966, I presented a paper at the American Marketing Association called "Marketing in the Year 2000."[66] I described push-and-pull communications and how we're going to do our shopping via a television set and a virtual department store. If you want to buy a drill, you click on Hardware and that shows Tools and you click on that and go deeper.[67]

When the RAND group founded Advanced Research Projects Agency Network (ARPANET) for scientists to share information in 1969, they could hardly have imagined the vast expanse of social and commerce that is today networked globally by the click of a button.

So what kinds of churches will we see living and moving in the Western world in the future? What kinds of communities will reach the multiethnic, multilingual people who inhabit our mission context? How will these congregations inhabit the suburban and urban environments of tomorrow?

Let's apply Paul Baran's concept to the church for a moment. The church we inherit is primarily a centralized model. It is hierarchical in nature, true enough, but it is basically organized in this centralized manner. People come to a central point, the church. There they are ministered to, and there they receive programs, sacraments, and pastoral care. Sometimes the priest or ministers will travel out to the parishioner's home or to their workplaces or hospitals. It is essentially a centralized model of community that itself may have several levels of similarly working parts.

Figure 4. Current church model, centralized.

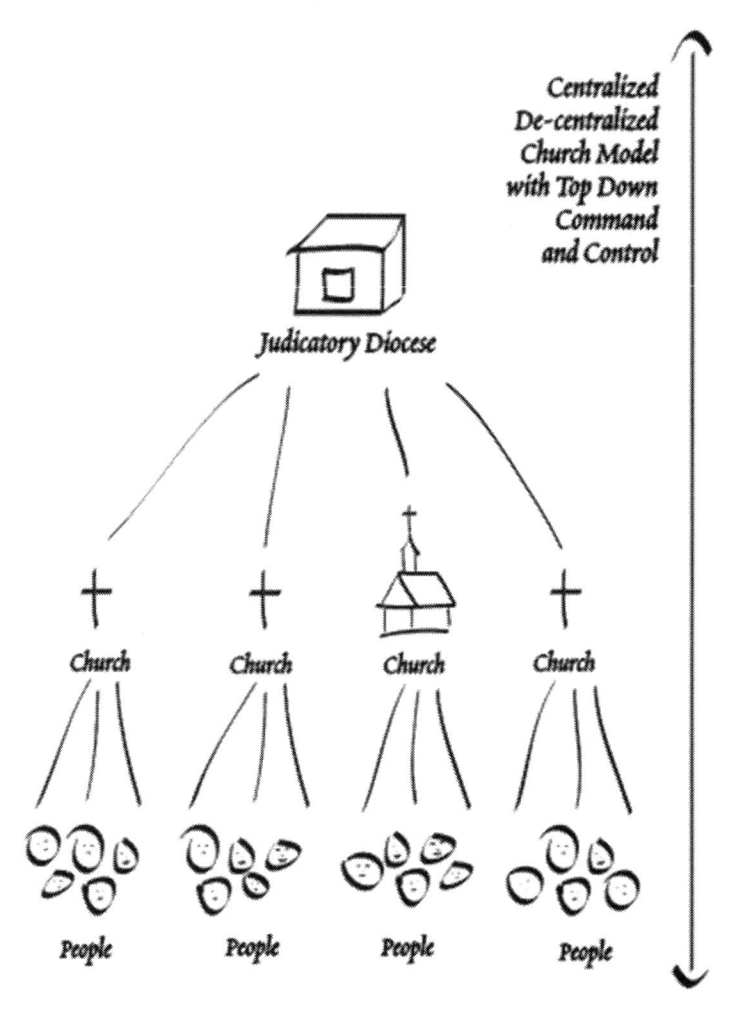

Centralized De-centralized Church Model with Top Down Command and Control

Judicatory Diocese

Church Church Church Church

People People People People

We have made large strides toward a more decentralized model. We have done this primarily at the higher levels of the organization. Yet even in the parish, there has been some substantial movement through the growth of programming ministries in the 1990s that created decentralized systems. Yet it is not a far-fetched thing to walk into a small parish in a small town and see a centralized system at work. In many ways, both the centralized and decentralized ideas of organization might be found in Rothauge's work around pastoral, program, and corporate congregations. (In later years a transitional stage was included, and "corporate" was changed to "resource.")

The form the missionary church will take in the future can be found in the artifact of the Internet and distributive system thinking. We are a weak organization today because we still believe that everyone must come to the same center. When that center is disrupted (for whatever reason ... and there are many), the system is weakened and can even die. There are models where the decentralized system is working well. I believe though, in order to engage with the culture, we are going to need a distributive system of mission.

A distributive system of mission creates multiple communities connected together. These communities are of different kinds, and they do different things. They share information that they collect from the organization. They then multiply it through their own webs of connections. A distributive mission doesn't store everything in one place. In other words, a distributive system is not a bunch of centralized systems connected. It uses what it needs within the particular context of ministry. It then shares with others what it learns and receives from others what it needs to be successful.

Figure 5. A disbursement model of a networked future church.

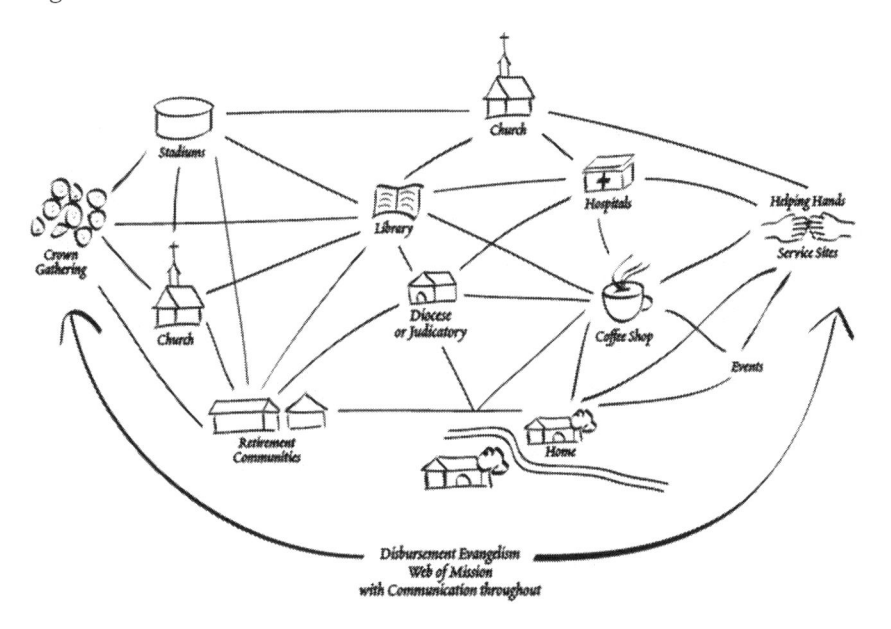

When I graduated from seminary in 1995, we used to say that big churches were getting bigger and small churches were dying. That is not quite true today. Every church, regardless of size, needs to move to a more distributive model of ministry. The church will find itself part of a web of relationships throughout its interdependent context. In the future, we will still have churches like we have them today. They will be of every size. They will be connected to parts of their communities. However, we will also have many more small batch Christian communities than we ever imagined. They will be one network node within the larger churchwide system. They will also be one network node within the worldwide network.

Dispatches from the Front: The Abbey

The Reverend Katie Nakamura Rengers is the founder of the Abbey Coffee Shop, a missional community in the Avondale neighborhood in Birmingham, Alabama. You can make your online pilgrim journey to the Abbey on the web here, http://www.theabbeybham.com. *This is their story.*

"Hospitality and conversation" are how they described the mission of their community. During the week, they run a coffee shop. On Sundays and some weeknights, they meet for worship in the Episcopal tradition. They consider the coffee shop to be just as significant in their identity as a church as the worship.

The Abbey coffee shop has been open about two months at the time of this writing. The worshipping community has been meeting for over seven months. Paid staff, including a manager who is paid by the diocese, run the coffee shop. The vicar and council of the worshipping community oversee finances, create programs, and develop neighborhood and diocesan relationships. The vicar and deacon occasionally take shifts behind the espresso machine, and their warden helps out with any repairs or other building needs.

The worshipping community meets on Sundays at 4:00 p.m. They typically have twelve to fifteen worshippers. The liturgy uses resources from the BCP, Enriching our Worship, and the Iona Abbey prayer book. They usually have a conversation-style sermon. The vicar or deacon poses a question based on the day's readings and invites the congregation into the homily.

> Katie says,
> I'm not sure how theologically astute these conversation sermons are ... the real advantage has been that they serve as a icebreaker for the community. In other words, there's none of that usual awkwardness after the dismissal when everyone is packing up to leave. They have already talked to each other during the sermon, and that friendliness continues after the service is over. It seems to fit in with our mission of hospitality and conversation.

How It Began

Avondale is an up-and-coming neighborhood and part of a wider rejuvenation going on in the city. The surrounding communities are becoming home to more and more young professionals, single and married and gay and straight. About three years ago, the diocese attempted about a nine-month "church without walls." For many reasons, this was a false start. That was okay and important because it reminds us that not everything works the first time. What is important is that the area was ripe for the small batch and the diocese continued to imagine what might go there.

Meanwhile Katie Rengers went off to the Church Planter's Academy in Minneapolis. She began to dream about this community. The stories she heard at the academy all had one significant thing in common. The missional communities that worked were the ones that attempted to exist differently than traditional churches. She heard from pastors who had started coffee shops, yoga studios, and dinner churches. They were all houses of prayer, but they made themselves available to the wider community in interesting ways.

In Alabama, they are reaping the last benefits of being a Bible Belt state, as are many Southern states. People will still come through the church doors just because they are looking for a place to go to church. But if you look forward twenty to thirty years, that attractional way of existing may, in fact, follow the trajectory of church attendance elsewhere in the country. It seemed to Rengers, "as the world moves away from religion, the Church needs to move deeper into the world." She believes we as a missional people need to create more opportunities for people to come into contact with the Christian community during the course of their everyday lives. "A yoga studio wouldn't go over in Birmingham … but a coffee shop would," she thought, and so the Abbey idea began to grow.

The Abbey applied for and received a First Mark of Mission grant from the National Church. To match the hundred thousand-dollar grant, the Diocese of Alabama agreed to pay the salary of our coffee shop manager, and Saint Luke's Episcopal Church agreed to keep paying Rengers's salary. They started an Indiegogo campaign and raised another forty thousand dollars to purchase equipment. The diocese also loaned them forty thousand dollars to help with build-out, architect's fees, furniture, and so forth.

Interestingly she did not originally conceive of the Abbey as having its own worshipping community. She thought of it more like a diocesan camp, a communal family space for the whole diocese to share. Within a few months, however, a number of people had started asking, "When are we going to start?" The desire for a new sort of worshipping community was evident, so they began holding weekly services in the big, empty space.

And today the worshipping community meets in the back of the coffee shop, while customers can sit at tables in the front.

What They Learned

1. Trust God. Trust God. Trust God. There have been at least a dozen significant moments when they were certain the entire Abbey project was about to come crashing down on their heads: getting the lease signed, raising money, enduring spats among community members, and getting through snowy days when the shop made no money. But they believed that God wanted the church to live, thrive, and reinvent itself, and the Abbey is playing a small role in that in their part of the world. At the same time, they don't think that God thinks of mission as being cheap, fast, or easy, so they couldn't expect it to be either.
2. Don't box it in! Little about their original ministry plan went according to plan, but everything was led by the Spirit.
3. Communicate! One of their biggest challenges at the beginning was lack of communication among all the interested parties. First was the problem that this had never been done before. There was no parochial or diocesan protocol for how to deal with new ideas, so they were not given any instruction on how to navigate the great bureaucracy that is the Episcopal Church. This is typical of many of the people I interviewed. And as a bishop, I am aware of this in our own office. This is a vestige of a time when the institution could trust uniformity as the primary overarching rule. The Abbey, like so many other small batch ministries, has forged a bit of a path through the jungle so other new ministries can find their way through.
4. They felt, for the Abbey to succeed, the vision had to be bottom-up. They wanted younger voices to be heard, and they didn't want anyone to butt in and ruin things. It is important to have clear boundaries earlier with clarity about vision before launch, if it is a community-sent from a congregation.

What They Might Do Differently

They wish they had built a stronger, more efficient ministry team at the beginning. They wanted (and still want) the Abbey to primarily be an outreach to younger adults. They thought this meant that younger adults should form the core of the ministry team, that is, younger people came up with the vision, designed the space, and executed the plan.

The problem is that most young adults have little experience with being on vestries, working with builders and architects, or thinking about church finances. Their team was great for bouncing around theological ideas, but not so good at executing the vision.

The Reimagining the Episcopal Church Group published a report that suggests the creation of regional committees of Episcopal architects, builders, and developers who could help churches reimagine and reinvent their space for the twenty-first century will be an essential ingredient of asset sharing within the missionary-focused diocese. Such a resource would have been invaluable if it had existed as they were building the Abbey. Perhaps it wouldn't be a bad idea to add a committee of accountants and small business owners as well, those who would offer pro bono services to new ministry endeavors. If people of faith were willing to offer their professional expertise to new ministry starts, not usurping but strengthening the vision, wow![68]

Questions

1. Bishop Doyle says we have "created a system by which people support the church rather than the church support the people in making community." Do you agree with his observation? Why or why not?
2. Consider the church you currently attend. What space has been or could be repurposed to create what Doyle calls a culture of sharing grace?
3. What do you think the difference is between a centralized and distributed network? Do you believe that the future Episcopal Church will embrace a more distributive model?
4. "The Episcopal Church is dying." After reading this chapter, in what sense is this statement true? In what sense is it not a true statement to say that the church is dying?

Recommendations for Further Reading

Church in the Inventive Age by Doug Pagitt

The Great Emergence by Phyllis Tickle

Chapter 4

The Birth of Vitality and Mission Amplification

Procrustes, a character whose name means "he who stretches," was arguably the most interesting of Theseus's challenges on the way to becoming a hero. He kept a house by the side of the road where he offered hospitality to passing strangers, who were invited in for a pleasant meal and a night's rest in his very special iron bed. Procrustes described it as having the unique property that its length exactly matched whoever lay down upon it. What Procrustes didn't volunteer was the method by which this "one size fits all" was achieved. Namely as soon as the guest lay down, Procrustes went to work upon him, stretching him on the rack if he were too short for the bed and chopping off his legs if he were too long. Theseus turned the tables on Procrustes, fatally adjusting him to fit his own bed.

Nassim Taleb, in his book *Black Swan*, amplifies theories regarding the reality that randomness and variability are very real participants in making history. He says, "History is opaque. You see what comes out, not the script that produces events ... The generator of historical events is different from the events themselves, much as the minds of the gods cannot be read just by witnessing their deeds."[69] He also explains the reality that we have difficulty not categorizing everything. He says,

> Because our minds need to reduce information, we are more likely to try to squeeze a phenomenon into the Procrustean bed[70] of a crisp and known category (amputating the unknown), rather than suspend categorization, and make it tangible. Thanks to our detections of false patterns, along with real ones, what is random

will appear less random and more certain—our overactive brains are more likely to impose the wrong, simplistic, narrative than no narrative at all.[71]

Clear as mud? Did he just use Procrustean bed in a sentence? Congregational development is a Procrustean bed. Congregational development is the application of congregational sizes and theories to programs. It is based upon a proposition of history that is first of all centered in the unusual period of church attendance that lasted for a little over seventy of Christianity's two thousand years. It is based upon a particular matrix that makes up that time period, categorized congregations based upon large statistical averages, and what appeared to be the results of particular habits, separate from the reality of context. Some of this observation bias misses the contextual factors of the time, a lack of competition by media or social activities; a mass movement of a religiously oriented and uniquely church-focused generation; and a context that included the building of massive bureaucracies, clubs, and institutions like no other time in history. Well into the last decade, we have continued to apply the WYSIATI applications to congregations and the work of mission while the end results have not supported the efforts and theories.

What we have come to know is that it is a new period of time, a new context, a complex time that will take new structures and organizations to serve the mission of the church in a new era. Behold the death of congregational development.

Our work in the area of community and congregational life isn't about application of program or a procrustean bed of congregational development; rather it's about community and congregational vitality. It is about an amplification of gifts for the work of mission. It is too easy to group congregations into contextual, economic, and leadership systems that are not their own. It is easy to believe that the work of the church is the work of developing congregations. We want to amplify through the planting and health of communities and congregations, the mission of God, the *Missio Dei*.

Vision for Transformation toward healthy communities

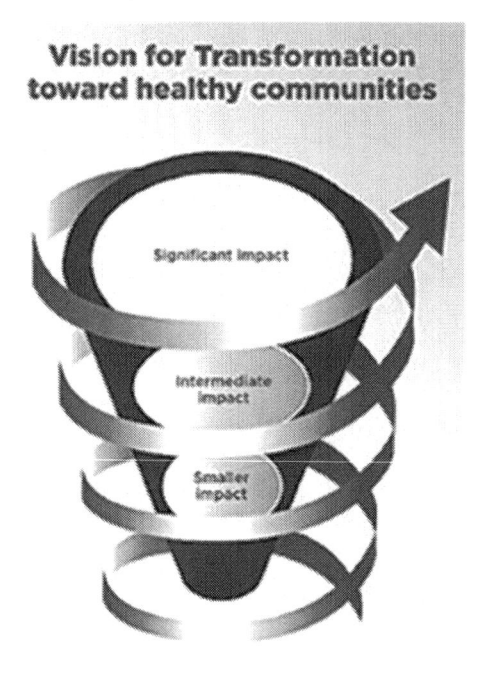

Significant impact

Intermediate impact

Smaller impact

We believe that God's mission is reconciliation. God in Christ Jesus has reconciled the world and us to himself and to one another. God's mission has a church. Our work is to undertake the mission of reconciliation through service and evangelism. While the Episcopal Health Foundation in the Diocese of Texas seeks to lead our churches in the work of mission, service, and servanthood, it is the work of the mission amplification office to lead our churches in the work of evangelism. We define evangelism as sharing the gospel/Good News of God's reconciling work. We do this by creating and expanding the safe and peaceful space where people may discover God's love and forgiveness, where we live with difference and celebrate diversity, and where we help to heal history. We believe we are being successful when people are discovering Jesus Christ in the power of the Holy Spirit through our work and people are coming to trust in God through the revelation and work of Jesus such that they accept him as Savior and begin to seek a closer relationship with him through the fellowship in the church and join us in service to our community. We believe we are accomplishing this work when we are grace-filled and grace-sharing communities.

We believe this is the work of transformation and model it in this way whether we are speaking about the work of service or evangelism. Healthy communities begin their work with small relational coaching and collaborations. Healthy communities work on short-term goals and scenarios, building strength across the organization.

The work of the mission amplification is to aid communities and congregations to achieve their potential given their mission context. Not every context has people moving into it. Some are in small towns, others are in urban areas, and still others are suburban. Each has a unique demographic and makeup.

Figure 6. This concept of foresight is from the Institute for the Future. Their concept helps us understand how to look at opportunities for mission.

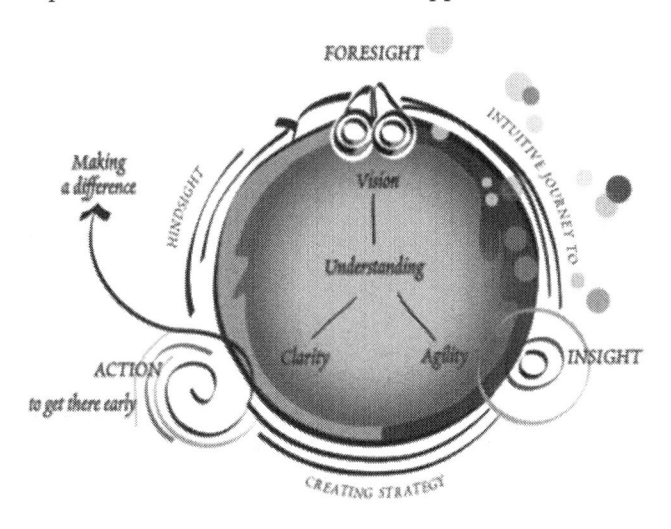

Mission amplification will be done by creating a structure of coaching and collaboration, resource sharing, and case management. We have assets and human resources for the undertaking of God's mission, and we must seek to make better strategic use of our collaborative investments of time, money, and gifts. We are not focused on the congregation but upon the discernment of gifts that serve God's mission.

We also believe that we need to look at the future.[72] The future developments within our communities and contexts offer important clues to the potential mission work we must undertake. To do this, we use foresight. Think of it like a foresight engine. We cycle through a process of gaining insight that leads to action. We look at the present and future trends in the culture and gain insight from their trajectories. This then leads to strategy based on context. This leads to action with a different outcome. These outcomes then may be reviewed and the process reworked.

This means looking at cultural, demographic, and contextual trends to help gain insight into the shaping of future. While the world is a VUCA world, the working of the foresight engine enables us to gain vision, understanding, clarity, and ability. Our intuitive journeys into the future lead to insight that helps us build and create a strategy. Action through our theories and strategies then brings hindsight and enables us to relook at the future from a new position.

We believe, when we do this, we are empowering and connecting people first and then resources and assets across a diocesan community. In turn we are creating, adding to, and sustaining a network of relationships and common work. Modeled on Baran's work to create a disbursed system, which eventually became the basics for the Internet, we build a network of strength using our difference and diversity as an interlocking web. Failure of any one node does not create a system cascade into chaos or a system failure.[73] Furthermore the whole system is able to grow and adapt based upon its neighbors' insights. This is the work of creating a diverse community of Christian communities, or commons, where we are driving deep into the organization a long-lasting, antifragile DNA.

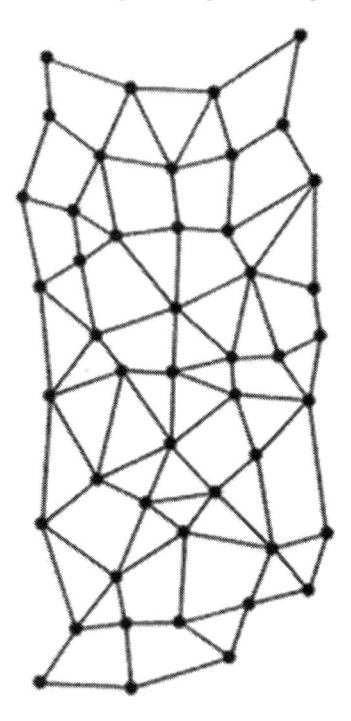

This leads to a cycle of innovation and creativity. Within any one node, we can work on the particular context and build a ministry plan using the insight engine. As we do this, we are literally amplifying and focusing upon the mission. A graphic for the cycle of innovation helps us see the application of the insight engine. This cycle helps to amplify. When we lay this over the insight engine, we see that what we are doing is building a creative cycle.[74]

The work of mission amplification is to press the assets (human, financial, or physical) into this work. We must reflect and manage the process, constantly adjusting and investing in the mission amplification theories. Mission amplification is not a lone ranger work but a team approach where coaching and collaboration are used to build cooperative and focused ministry in tandem.

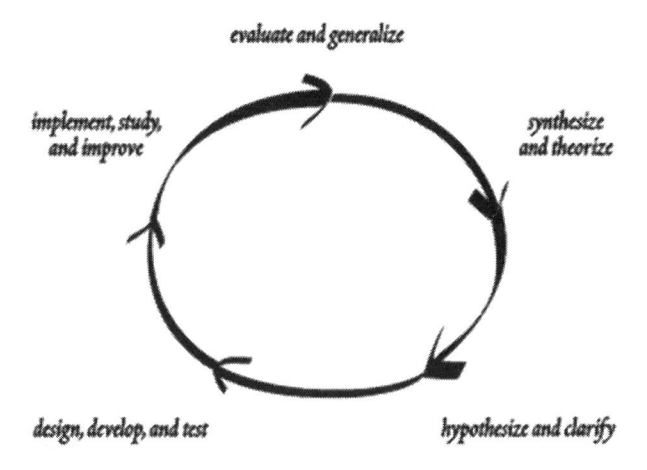

evaluate and generalize

implement, study, and improve *synthesize and theorize*

design, develop, and test *hypothesize and clarify*

As any one node does this, it is important to reflect and share information across the network. This is artificially created through old super bureaucracies today, but these will, over time, give way for emerging natural networks that will live, sustain, and pass away as needed. As a diocese, we know that this will mean moving assets across the spectrum of strategic innovation in order to maximize our work. This is true in the local congregation.

Strategy

Low Risk ← **Downstream** <Transactional>
- Low risk
- Immediate impact
- Service delivery projects
- Capacity building

Intermediate <Transitional>
- Intermediate risk
- Longer time horizon
- Known outcome
- Results over a period of time

Upstream <Transformational>
- High risk/return
- Long-term investment
- Innovative
- Ignores need to address present concerns

→ High Risk

In the current congregational model, we spend most of our time trying to build impacts on the left side of the spectrum. With few resources, a tentative model with limited success, and a complex context, we are left to try to conserve and make change happen that is predictable. When we open ourselves up to see that we have unlimited resources in terms of human power, time, energy, and gifts. And add this to our present financial and physical assets, mission amplification begins to move and shape ministry through the above engines across this horizon moving from the secure predictable win downstream to the upstream transformational work, which is a high-risk return, long-term investment that is innovative and leap-frogs beyond the present concerns.

Seeing our system, flattening our hierarchy, understanding assets, and using this to leverage momentum through collaborative coaching helps to move out of the internally focused congregation into a mission commons where we are adapting and emerging within the culture. This will, in turn, create socially structured communities. The networks of congregations/communities, human resources, social media, and space build a new multidimensional model of a new commons. Futurist Marina Gorbis writes,

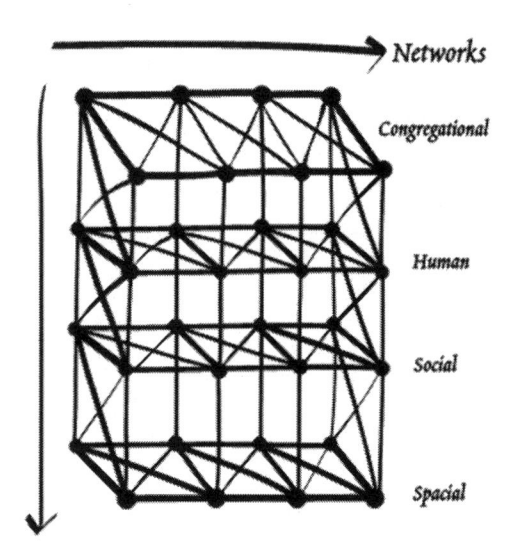

New Multi Dimensional Commons

> The transactions facilitated by social platforms are creating a different kind of value and a different kind of wealth, which is not necessarily measurable in monetary terms. This wealth is in part a matter of how we feel when we engage in these

transactions. Socially embedded transactions increase our levels of connectedness and engagement with others.[75]

Jonathan Haidt, professor of psychology at the University of Virginia, writes,

> We are, in a way, like bees: our lives only make full sense as members of a larger hive, or as cells in a larger body. Yet in our modern way of living we've busted out of the hive and flown out on our own, each one of us free to live as we please. Most of us need to be part of a hive in some way, ideally a hive that has a clearly noble purpose.[76]

It turns out that our very happiness may actually be rooted in how well we are connected and how much we spend and give to others.[77]

In 2010 I read an important book by Clay Shirky, *Cognitive Surplus*. In it, he says, since 1940, there has been an exponential increase in free time. (This is not unlike what I argued in terms of average Sunday attendance.) There are many more opportunities for us to use our free time today, perhaps more than ever. He would argue that we have more opportunity to be creative and collaborative. The time we have to contribute is growing, and we as individuals are participating across many new portals and in many new projects.

Shirky, like myself, grew up consuming large amounts of television; in fact we watched a lot of the same shows. Today my daughter has several creative sites that she runs with literally hundreds of participants sharing ideas with her and she with them. We are, according to Shirky, creating a new era of human expression. Marina Gorbis, in her work on the nature of the future, says that digital natives, people who have always known technology (think two-year-olds who know how to navigate an iPad) versus those of us who had to learn it, are now sharing themselves across a multitude of platforms, giving and sharing ideas and money in a new more socially connected universe. We are doing a lot of this work, using our cognitive surplus without receiving what is essential in modern economies, monetary rewards.[78] The question for the church is, "What kind of surplus do we have that might be networked with this wider global movement?" The answer is the stewardship of our relationships. The living and thriving future church will participate in this global evolution by using its surplus of connected individuals and communities across the globe for the sake of mission.

We need a targeted strategy around turnarounds and places where we can coach and collaborate for easy wins. This is to make an effort to do the downstream work. We need to look at areas where we can leverage resources and restructure for value-driven transformative change. This will mean truly understanding leadership and group needs per congregation. We want to be clear about where we have opportunities for active driving change and where we are doing the work of caring pastorally for the congregation. Each congregation goes through seasons. We must be aware enough of the seasons of congregations in order to not waste assets during a season of passivity. We are constantly looking for the leverage points and the opportunities for transformative change that lead to long-term goals. We must always remember, in the long life of congregations, as my friend Caesar Kalinowski says, "fast is slow" and "small is big."[79]

We are working a mixed, diverse strategy. In our mission toolbox are the vast resources of human capital: time, experience, and creativity. Understanding and knowing the breadth of leadership gifts and opportunities for leveraging human innovative power in this system will be one of the keys to success. Also there will be the understanding that we believe in a system approach. We know that this network of relationships across the diocese and within a congregation is a system. Therefore the system is to be systematically invested in with a strategy of maximizing impact. I believe this will bring slow but exponential growth in mission.

Dispatches from the Front: Veterans Fellowship

The Episcopal Veterans Fellowship (EVF) is a group of women and men on the long journey home from war. This fellowship exists in some places as an extension of the congregation, a greenfield. In other instances we see this emerging as a stand-alone community, a missional community that focuses on healing the spiritual wounds of war through pilgrimages of reconciliation, trust-filled community groups, and the ancient practice of lament. The ultimate purpose is to form a community that understands their own spiritual journey in war and homecoming. From that understanding, a renewed connection to Christ and his church can form. Currently we have four groups meeting in four parishes in Central Texas.

This is how it began.

EVF was born out of its founder's own struggles with coming home from the war in Iraq. When David Peters first arrived home, he tried to get back to normal life. This soon proved to be impossible. Relationships and beliefs began to shatter. In reality they were already gone in Iraq. It just took him a long time to realize his loss. The worst part of this time was the loss of his relationship with God. He felt betrayed by God, and his symptoms of anger and numbness intensified. He didn't realize he wasn't alone in his struggle, mainly because he didn't trust anyone enough to tell them how disturbed he was.

When he finally left active duty in the US Army, he moved to Texas, where thousands of veterans of Iraq and Afghanistan were enduring the trials of homecoming themselves. After hearing their stories and finding how they sounded much like his own, he began to build relationships with them and think about how the church could meet the spiritual needs of this community. The primary need for this community was reconciliation with themselves, God, and the church community that sent them to war. Drawing from his experience with pilgrimages to the National Cathedral, he developed a liturgy for veterans to bring their combat experiences to the altar.

Armed with this basic idea for a veterans ministry, he accompanied a retired army chaplain, The Reverend David Scheider, to meet with me about starting a veterans ministry. I encouraged them both. He recalls my emphasis on community building, which eventually became the grounding principle of the EVF. Armed with this commission and a dream, David applied for a grant from the Episcopal Evangelism Society. Their generous gift of five thousand dollars provided the final nudge to step out and start something.

Their first meeting was a pilgrimage of remembrance and reconciliation at St. David's Church, a downtown parish in Austin. They advertised on the radio and tried to get the word out about the new group. Eight people came to the first meeting, and the group was born. From the beginning the veterans who attended this first meeting have formed the leadership circle of the group. Peters's original vision was to conduct literal pilgrimages, hikes from St. David's to war memorials in the Austin area. After the first meeting, the veterans, especially the Vietnam and World War II veterans, made it very clear that they weren't interested in any physical activity, especially since it was summer in Austin with temperatures in the upper nineties. Naturally he was disappointed. After all it was the pilgrimage model that he envisioned in the long months of preparation. They were, however, interested in meeting together and building community. Hmmmm …

They started off their meetings with snacks or a meal as well as an honest check-in. He quickly found that his own vulnerability about his struggles offered an invitation for others to be open about theirs. Referrals to mental health professionals and other resources were an integral part of the check-in. Next he facilitated a discussion that addressed the spiritual dimensions of war and homecoming. This was followed by a time of lament, where veterans shared a poem, a song, or another work of art that captured their feelings and experiences. Finally they prayed the Compline Office, a short prayer service infused with military themes of protection and safety. At the writing of this book, this model has replicated itself in three other parishes that currently have EVF groups.

What They Learned

Through this process David learned he had to listen carefully to discern the needs of the community, no matter what his needs and visions were at the time. He also learned the power of laypersons to start their own groups and carry the ministry into the world. He started the first two groups with key support from then-Deacon Robert Chambers, the son of a Korean War veteran, and Episcopal seminarian Lynn Smith-Henry, an Army veteran. These two men provided the early community for David. The second two groups were started by motivated laypersons, Warren, Steve, and Robert. Steve leads a group at St. Christopher's in Killeen, Texas, the city that includes the world's largest military base, Fort Hood. He describes his community being "like the surface of Mars ... compared to other non-military communities."

In this unique environment, Steve and The Reverend Janice Jones, the parish rector, focus more on providing authentic community for active-duty soldiers and veterans, as well as family members and spouses. In this highly transient community, they recognized the needs and responded. Clergy support was key to the success of these additional groups. Veterans are used to a hierarchy of command and support, so without the rector's support, Peters found it impossible to form a group of veterans within the parish.

Starting anything new requires patience and a beginner's mind. Success is defined by a community that trusts each other and is doing the spiritual work of reconciliation themselves. The stories of reconciliation are astounding to all who hear them. On three occasions, veterans told Peters the group was responsible for saving their lives as they had planned their suicides. He learned that warriors aren't afraid of dying, but they are afraid of being alone. The group's effectiveness comes out of its safety. Laughter and tears are their indicators of whether participants feel safe.

During the time Peters was creating safety for the group, his own safety was difficult to maintain. The intense sharing of combat experiences in the group brought up many of his own memories, and the symptoms followed. He soon realized that he had to engage his own issues with war and homecoming if he were to be of any use to the community. He began attending a group at the VA hospital and other counseling appointments.

This helped him process his own issues so he could continue leading the community.

What They Might Do Differently

If he were to do anything differently, David says he would have found lay leaders earlier and spent more time with them, preparing them for the ministry. His worries about well-meaning folk hijacking the group were mostly unfounded, but those worries made it difficult for him to share the vision with others. "More trust in God, less fear of failure, is a succinct account of what I learned," he wrote.[80]

Questions

1. What do you see as the main difference between congregational development and mission amplification? How might an emphasis on mission amplification be more useful in today's world?
2. Bishop Doyle says a commitment to foresight enables us to gain insight so the church might discern the most appropriate action. Do you agree? As you ponder the future world (foresight), what insight does that give you into God's call to today's church? What actions do you recommend that the church take based on your insight?
3. What does the phrase "stewardship of relationships" mean to you? What does it mean to steward relationships for the sake of mission amplification?
4. Bishop Doyle writes, "Mission amplification is not lone ranger work but a team approach." What changes must the church make to build more aligned and enthusiastic teams committed to common mission?

Recommendations for Further Reading

The Wisdom of Stability: Rooting Faith in a Mobile Culture by Jonathan Wilson-Hartgrove

Killing from the Inside Out: Moral Injury and Just War by Robert Meagher

attraction & sending

CHAPTER 5

Church and the Continuum of Mission

We have a way of doing church that can be thought of in two ways that I find helpful: attraction and sending. These will, in the end, help us understand the place of small batch communities in our mission toolbox.

The first thing is to understand that most of the ways in which we've been doing church over the last seventy years has been predominantly an attractional church model. Evangelism in an attractional church model sends out people to invite people to church. We now do that, of course, on websites and in a number of different ways, but for the most part, what you do is you send people out. But the sending out is always focused on bringing people to the attractional church. It is rarely to set up a new Christian community.

In the attractional church,[81] most of the people serve and spend most of their ministry time inside the church. A great example of this is a research piece that a friend of mine undertook when he wanted to measure the reality of this statement. He found out, in a congregation of about three hundred, it will take about thirty people to put on the services for Sunday morning. On high holy days, it takes over seventy.

At their best, the way the attractional church grows is by inviting people in, welcoming them, and connecting them to real ministry through the discernment of gifts. If we look at where people are really struggling, it's always around the ministry of invitation. Every Sunday, people choose our congregations, so doing the welcoming and connecting better will mean, where we have visitors, we will grow. But we must do the work of inviting too. Waiting for people to find us is an assumption long now faded from cultural practice.

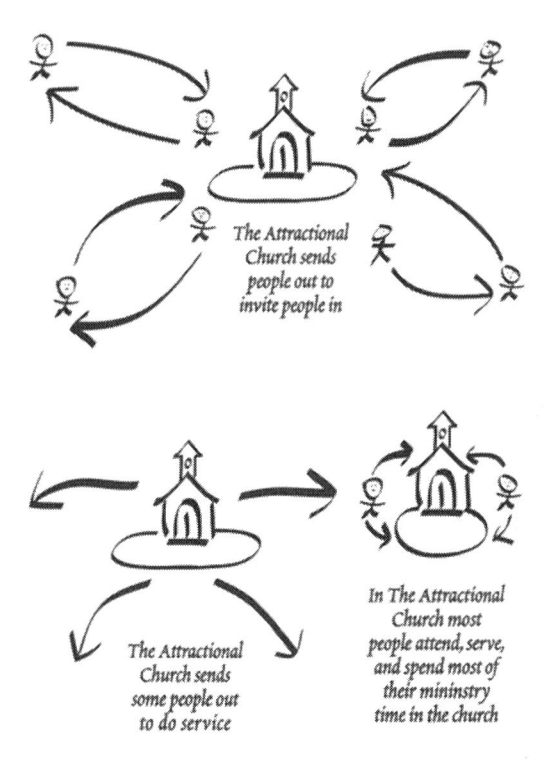

The Attractional Church sends people out to invite people in

The Attractional Church sends some people out to do service

In The Attractional Church most people attend, serve, and spend most of their mininstry time in the church

Think about the reality of what the ministries are in your congregation. I can predict, at the very bare minimum, they are Sunday school, lay Eucharistic ministers, readers, ushers, and altar guild. All of these are dominant ministries happening internally. Many are happening around the altar. It is true that the attractional church does send out some people to do service, and they may have service programs within the attractional church that they run themselves, or they may participate in other kinds of service, ways of reaching out into the community. This is the way that the attractional church works.

To increase health and vitality in an attractional church, you must diversify your ministries with meaningful relationship-oriented work. You must do the heavy lifting of discerning gifts for ministry instead of filling positions. And you must engage in inviting, welcoming, and connecting people into the community. What characterizes congregational vitality? Congregational vitality in the attractional church is modeled when a congregation is inviting, welcoming, and connecting people inside the church community and through greenfield ministries.

As we go deeper into understanding the future of evangelism and the attractional church and how it lives and moves, we discover it may send out people. One of the things that happens is that we learn more and more about this in the doing of the work. We have found that an attractional church may send out a group of people to start a greenfield ministry. Greenfields are attractional church Bible studies and ministries that are happening out in the world, but they are always connected to the attractional church. Their point of doing something is always to bring people back into the attractional church. It is to increase the doors of the church.

So the greenfield ministry really is not about leaving the church and becoming a separate Christian community of Episcopalians out in the world, serving other people in partnership with neighbors and other community members. It's really about creating another entry point for the attractional church. And so that's a very important distinguishing characteristic. Here when a person joins the Bible study in a pub and wants to become part of the community, he or she finds he or she is attracted into the life of the mother church.

A great example of a greenfield ministry is the Bible study begun by The Reverend Nick Novak in a mechanics garage. Their numbers have been small, nine or ten on a big night. Most would not be at a Bible study at the church, although a couple folks from the church found out we were doing it and decided to join in from time to time.

The location has a history. The shop is owned by Robert Jordan, the rector's best friend and sometime junior/senior warden at Trinity Church. Robert's shop has been a fixture in Baytown for decades, but what makes it unique is that it has for many years also been a place where significant ministry takes place. Novak writes,

> Robert is a cancer survivor a couple of times over and has encountered some rare forms of the disease and some radical treatment protocols that resulted from that. Because he beat significant odds, he has become a touchstone for people inside and outside the church and people who are newly diagnosed often come to him for encouragement and advice. I know for a fact that he has been contacted by perfect strangers from all over the country (we cancer people have our own coconut telegraph). It is not unusual to enter his shop and find people in prayer, in tears or in celebration. We refer to it around here as the Trinity South Campus. It's a holy place.

It is nothing less than a garage and has integrity because of the charity there and the working of the Holy Spirit that has accomplished some amazing things, so Nick and Robert thought it might be a good spot to begin a different kind of Bible study. They are of the mind-set, if only one person is drawn closer to the Lord through this effort, it will be worth it. Novak says, "I guess it would be fair to say we are planting a few seeds that may get watered down the road and that's good enough for now."

The difference between this greenfield and the small batch missional community is that it belongs to Trinity in a way. People who wish to may come along to church on Sunday. It is not meant as a particularly stand-alone ministry, though it certainly has many characteristics similar to other small batch communities in this book.

What we know is that some churches raise up individuals who feel a call to something different. They are called to go out and not come back. They are called to create a small batch ministry out in the world. Sometimes called tentmaker ministries, these are where people literally multiply Christian community by starting something new and different. These are people, hopefully through the discernment of gifts who discover they are called to go out and form communities with people who are not part of the existing sending community. In doing this the attractional church takes on an additional characteristic beyond greenfield planting. It becomes a sending church.

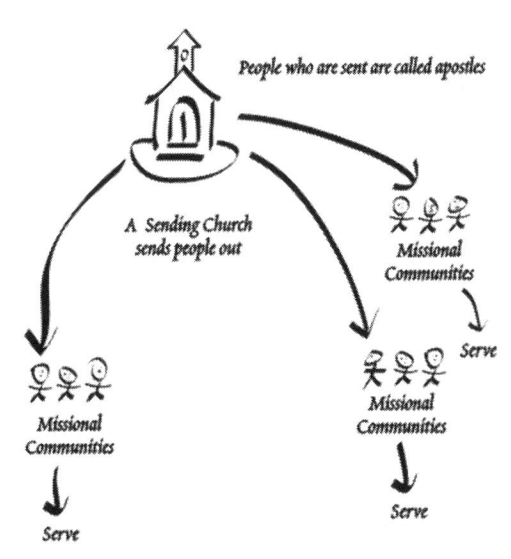

People who are sent are called apostles

A Sending Church sends people out

Missional Communities

Serve

- Missional Communities may (at times) return to Sending Church on feast & holy days, and to report on mission.
- Missional Communities have a worship life of their own. It may not be on Sunday.
- Most are led by lay pastoral leaders, lay evangelists, lay eucharistic ministers, and/or lay worship leaders.
- Missional Communities have clarity & focus around their common life & have a clear ministry.

Small Batch = local, sustainable, organic —

C. Andrew Doyle

A sending congregation sends people out. It raises up people to be disciples, followers of Jesus. We must remember that every disciple Jesus called to follow, he turned into an apostle and sent them out. Accordingly a sending church raises up apostles and sends them out. You can be a big or small community.

Sometimes we as leaders get stuck because we think we can't send out people to do ministry and start new communities until we are finished building our attractional church. I think this stumbling block happens out of a sense of scarcity or misunderstanding that God does the calling and sending out. If we hold back those who are feeling the Holy Spirit move and send them out, we are frustrating the work of the Holy Spirit.

The sending congregation is healthy not because of numbers or money. The sending congregation is healthy because it discerns and honors gifts and looks beyond itself out to the mission field and sees what Jesus saw. The sending church sees that the harvest is plentiful, and a faithful response is to send out laborers into the field.

What are the characteristics of congregational vitality in a sending church? Congregational vitality in a sending community is characterized by the amplification of mission by multiplying Christian communities in the world.

One of the things I really have come to understand and believe about the future of the church is that we have to create more and more doors to our churches, places where people come in contact with our ministry and our communities. A sending church then empowers and blesses a few individuals who are sent out of their community to create what we are calling "missional communities." These are small batch Christian communities. They are unburdened by the structures and overhead of the sending community so they are sustainable. They are lay-led and clergy-supported. They are made up of people coming from the church and individuals from the community, so they are uniquely local. Their full life of ministry is spent off the church property organically growing out of the relationships among the community members.

+ it multiplies itself —

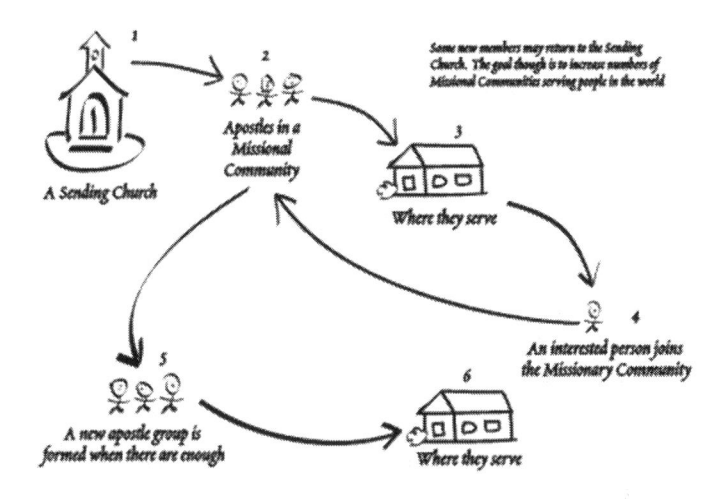

Some new members may return to the Sending Church. The goal though is to increase numbers of Missional Communities serving people in the world

1. A Sending Church
2. Apostles in a Missional Community
3. Where they serve
4. An interested person joins the Missionary Community
5. A new apostle group is formed when there are enough
6. Where they serve

Small batch missional communities probably serve in places like nursing homes. Maybe they've chosen a neighborhood in which to plant house churches. Maybe they've adopted a hospital in which they're going to provide all of the pastoral care and run worship services there. Maybe they have a particular group like homeless or elderly that they have adopted or maybe even a school. As they grow, if they become too big, one of the things they do is multiply themselves and choose another place in which to do ministry, perhaps another hospital, neighborhood, nursing home, and so forth. So the very nature of the small batch community is that it is local, organic, and sustainable, and it multiplies itself.

Going deeper and exploring the concepts, we might say that small batch missional communities are local because it is locally based in a neighborhood, community, or part of town. This local nature is steeped in the fabric of the community. Those sent recognize that the locale, food, music, and community interests are essential to reflect within the community itself. The community is organic because it grows up in the midst of the community. It is not genetically modified by the sending church DNA.

This is, in fact, the very character of Anglican mission. It takes with it the Bible, the sacraments, the prayer book, and the orders of ministry, but it is deeply at its best when it comes up from the roots planted in the local soil. This is how liturgy, music, and the manner of gathering reflect the very nature of the community in which it finds itself. The small batch missional community is also sustainable. By leveraging the sending church organization and structure, along with a leveraging of public or private space, it brings down the cost and overhead of the larger church plant models. Furthermore, because the small batch community depends on lay leadership and different forms of clergy support, it brings down the cost of staffing normally associated with the idea of church. In this way our new small batch communities are nimble and adaptive and able to multiply quickly, immersing themselves in the culture around them.

The missional community is focused on serving. It is figuring out how to be a neighbor to its surrounding community. As they serve, people will become interested in what is happening, and so they may ask or wonder. As they serve people, people may ask them who they are, and they'll say, "Well, we're part of this missional community. Would you like to join us? We serve this nursing home." So they become part of this ministry to the nursing home. Their purpose is not to send them back to the sending church. (That would be an attractional response to the question.) But it is to engage them in the ministry of service. This is as important as the idea that these are local, organic, and sustainable.

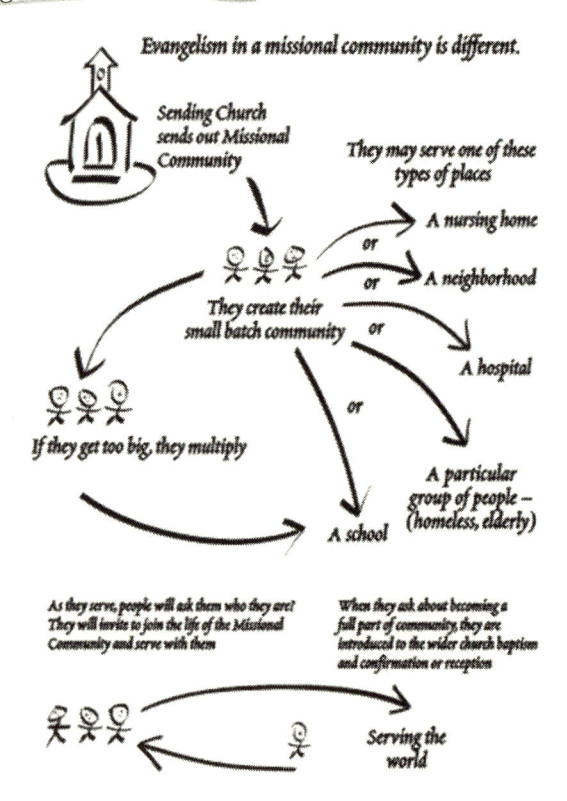

Evangelism in a missional community is different.

- Sending Church sends out Missional Community
- They create their small batch community
- They may serve one of these types of places
  - A nursing home
  - A neighborhood
  - A hospital
  - A particular group of people – (homeless, elderly)
  - A school
- If they get too big, they multiply
- As they serve, people will ask them who they are? They will invite to join the life of the Missional Community and serve with them
- When they ask about becoming a full part of community, they are introduced to the wider church baptism and confirmation or reception
- Serving the world

The model of small batch communities rejects the idea that you come into faith by teaching or using an old pedagogical model of Christian formation that begins with a book study or Bible class. The small batch missional community forms people first through service, as opposed to through program and liturgy.

Now as this new person engages the ministry of service and continues to join them in the serving and doing of the work in the wider community, they may then be led to ask, "Well, I notice you all are from the Abbey Episcopal Community, and I want to know more about that." So then a member of the community might say, "Yes, we meet each week for fellowship and dinner. We also pray together. Would you like to join us?" The person then might say yes.

So the second important step after showing new members how to serve is showing new members that the key to Christian life is a common meal together where friends gather. Again here is an important difference. I learned this from Caesar Kalinowski's work that fellowship and breaking bread together, partying together, is what Christian communities get to do.[82]

Only when the sending church comes up in the conversation might a member of a small batch community introduce a new person to the sending church. As most of their life is lived fully in the missional community, there is no need to go back to the sending church. However, from time to time, to report on the mission work or for feast days or festivals, they might return. I cannot stress enough that the full life of the church is lived out in these small batch locally grown, organic, and sustainable communities.

I imagine, in order to do this, most of these missional communities will be led by lay pastoral leaders, evangelists, Eucharistic ministers, and/or worship leaders. And they may have either a bivocational priest, a deacon, or even a regular priest who is making the rounds from the sending church to check in, help organize, support, and sustain their ministry, but they are predominantly not going to be led by people in funny collars.

So again, missional communities, as we send them out, will really be taking on this ministry. We begin to grow in our missional strength because the future of the church is embracing fully the ministry of the laity, and instead of being clergy-led and lay-supported, it is lay-led and clergy-supported. And if we think about this in a continuum of mission, we might discover that we move from chronic decline to sending and multiplying communities. Here is a chart that helps to parse out the characteristics and behaviors that differentiate the many different kinds of congregations. The deep task of congregations is to reclaim their mission work, to move from an internally focused attractional model to a sending church model. Any size community or congregation may become a sending and multiplying church.

Continuum of Mission

	Chronic Decline	Plateaued Attractional	Growing Attractional	Sending Church	Multiplying Church	Where Is Your Congregation?
Spiritual focus of Organization	Survival of Congregation	Satisfaction of the current congregation	Transformation through spiritual growth and service	Transformation of mission outward	Transformation of context	
Emotional Center of Gravity	satisfied, fearful, anxious, confused	"Club" atmosphere, members are cared for, clergy & lay pillars centered, nostalgia, loyalty, duty, commitment	Desire to share spiritual growth, adding programs for a variety of ages and interests, hope, expectancy	Embracing an Apostolic mission from following to going, Kingdom-ambition, or holy ambition	members are apostles, the world, community, neighborhood, joy, curiosity, wonder	
Core DNA	stagnation regarding growth, disengagement from wider community	predictable	bustling, busy, expanding	adventure, going, gathering, serving, partnerships	learning, multiplying, agility, organic, local, sustainable structures	
Behaviors	treading water, looking for quick-fix, asking for bail-out, reactive behavior, suspicion	few people do majority of work, commitment to the happiness of members, crowded calendar, liturgy designed for member preferences	goal-oriented leadership, high investment in liturgy and programming, skilled at newcomer attraction, invitation, and incorporation	visionary leader, dual focus on congregational vitality and mission, reproduction by addition	self-organize around core values, partner with community, team led	
#'s ($ & ASA)	ASA down, total pledges down, total budget down, average pledge up	ASA steady or in slow/imperceptible decline, average age and average pledge increase, funerals outpace baptisms	Often high growth with new rector, steady incremental growth, growing budget, decreasing average pledge + increasing ASA/membership, Greenfields, vision of 6/23 ministry	healthy enough to support 2nd site, missional communities, adult baptisms and confirmations increase and outpace funerals	metrics measure mission goals, structures are created only where needed for mission, low focus on ownership of property, budget is overwhelmingly mission support instead of overhead	
Downward Trajectory	Demise	Move into decline	Plateau when it hits limits to growth	Regress to attractional model, lose emphasis on mission	loss of identity, disintegration	
Potential	Stabilize as bi-vocational congregation and repurpose space for mission; liquidate assets for mission	Make internal changes needed for growth	capital campaign for campus growth, growth off campus with Greenfields and ministries oriented towards bringing outsiders in	Detach from daughter ministry, rest, and plan next missional adventure	growth and mitosis; multiplication, coach and partner with growing and sending church communities	
Reversal Requires	contextual health and growth, willingness to change habits and behaviors	building relationships in external/wider community, willingness to change habits and behaviors	Continued growth will require becoming a sending church: sending to invite, sending to plant, sending to gather, sending to work.	Doing it; actually going out and trying new & missional work, expecting both failure & "success."	Only continued & reinforced education that the work of the Church is in the World and not in a building will sustain the missional church	
Coaching Needed for change	Abundance vs Scarcity - theological sea change, see gifts and resources (including property) as God's assets for mission	Shared, distributive, new/rotating lay leadership, leadership focus on relationships outside of congregation, community partnerships are developed, emphasize quality over quantity	Focused leadership on core mission vs. doing/being all things for all people. Focusing on the programs that foster mission while jettisoning others.	Discernment as to mission field, places to try missional communities, growing partnerships outside of congregation	Support & encouragement for swimming as an "odd duck" in a sea of metrics, buildings, etc.	

The other day I was watching the *Steve Jobs* movie. There is a mythic scene where Steve Jobs is speaking with Steve Wozniak in an orchestra pit just before the launch of the NEXT computer. They are having one of their epic fights. In the movie Wozniak is upset because he feels like the engineers don't get enough credit. Steve Jobs is being more than a little bit of a jerk. Jobs is refusing to recognize the Apple team. Here is the conversation from the movie:

> Steve Jobs: How many fourth graders have heard of you?
>
> Steve Wozniak: You can't write code … you're not an engineer … you're not a designer … you can't put a hammer to a nail. I built the circuit board. The graphical interface was stolen from Xerox Parc. Jef Raskin was the leader of the Mac team before you threw him off his own project! Someone else designed the box! So how come ten times in a day, I read Steve Jobs is a genius? What do you do?
>
> Steve Jobs: I play the orchestra, and you're a good musician. You sit right there and you're the best in your row.

These two have been frenemies for a long time. But here is a metaphor embedded in their conversation that seems worth pondering in terms of the emerging mission patterns. The congregational model we have inherited, we have used for about sixty years or so. It is just one instrument in the mission of God. It is true that there are very real ways to bring forth the very best music out of a congregation. Those of us invested in this work should be using the continuum of mission and coaching to achieve the very best from this model. However, we must not forget that the Lord will raise up voices from stones and create a whole chorus of mission. The churchwide mission must be an orchestra seeking to bring forth a variety of beautiful sounds that will all sing, with harmonies, the song of the mission of God. We cannot be frenemies like Jobs and Wozniak. We are invited by the grace of God to work together, hand in hand, with our diverse gifts to serve the single mission of reconciliation. We as leaders are to be those conductors who bring forth the very best music from each chair from each type of community. In larger and healthier communities, we are to be the conductor multiplying the instruments in the orchestra. We no longer may simply play a single instrument and expect the world to hear a symphony.

Dispatches from the Front: Brotherhood of St. Andrew Prison Community

Before small batch was cool, Oliver Glass, a layperson at St. Timothy's Episcopal Church, started a Brotherhood of St. Andrew community inside the Wayne Scott Unit near Angleton, Texas. This is an attractional church that has created a very real missional community within a prison. *This is their story.*

St. Timothy's Episcopal Church in Lake Jackson established and supports an unofficial chapter of the Brotherhood of St. Andrew in a state prison nearby, the Wayne Scott Unit near Angleton. The chapter is unofficial in the sense that the incarcerated members are not able to pay annual dues, but in terms of sheer numbers, it is the largest chapter of the Brotherhood in the United States. This missional community at the prison pursues the stated mission of the greater Brotherhood organization to spread Christ's kingdom among men and boys.

Every Sunday afternoon, one of the missioners on a five-member team goes out to the prison to spend ninety minutes with four to six inmates in the Trusty Camp. Then it's another ninety minutes with thirty to fifty inmates in the main unit. Each meeting begins with the opening devotions of the Brotherhood. The missioner makes a presentation, often based upon a book, and elicits discussion. The men are invited to offer their testimony regarding how they've seen Christ in their lives recently. The meeting concludes in prayer.

Further, every August for the past nine years, the Brotherhood chapter at St. Timothy's has held a retreat at the prison, beginning on a Friday evening and extending until late Saturday afternoon. The retreat features speakers (such as a national officer of the Brotherhood, Episcopal priests, or bishops), testimonies of inmates and visitors, discussion in small family groups, worship, and live music, along with plenty of homemade cookies, fruit, and other snacks. The annual retreat typically draws one hundred and fifty inmates, and many of these men, as a result, become regulars at the weekly meeting.

How It Began

A parishioner of St. Timothy's, Oliver Osborn, was invited after his retirement in 1982 to attend a Bill Glass crusade at a state prison near Palestine, Texas. During the event, three young prisoners asked Oliver to tell them about Jesus. He felt completely unprepared, but he did his best.

The next year, Oliver and a second parishioner, Tom McKeand, attended another Bill Glass event at the Wayne Scott Unit. They followed up by offering the prisoners a six-week Bible study, assisted by two more members of St. Timothy's Brotherhood. At some point, the prison chaplain asked them, "Where do you come from?" When he heard their answer, he hit upon the idea of organizing a chapter of the Brotherhood for the inmates. When this chaplain retired, St. Timothy's Brothers assumed leadership.

What They Learned

The missioners say they have learned that the Holy Spirit can be trusted to show up. Wherever two or three are gathered in Jesus's name, he is in the midst of them. Christ's community is not bounded and extends inside and outside the walls of the prison. They no longer even see the white uniforms on the inmates. And they find they want to enter the prison to see their friends inside since these friends can't come outside to see them. They testify to seeing inmates display great compassion, care, generosity, and unselfishness toward one another, and they acknowledge they are blessed by the prisoners, even more than they might be a blessing to them. The leaders have been moved by other men's willingness to be vulnerable and to shed tears.

What They Might Do Differently

One brother would like to see a Brotherhood meeting at the prison every Wednesday as well as every Sunday, but others are concerned about having enough manpower for that.

Questions

1. What do you see as the main difference between an attractional church and a missional community?
2. Bishop Doyle offers a continuum of mission chart to help identify the behaviors of different congregations with respect to mission. What do you find most useful about Doyle's continuum of mission chart? What do you find most challenging? Where would you place your congregation on the continuum of mission?
3. What strengths might an attractional church have that a small batch community lacks? What strengths might a small batch community have that an attractional church lacks?

4. What is the difference between how attractional churches and missional communities evangelize? Which form of evangelism is more consistent with your theology?

Recommendations for Further Reading

Practicing Our Faith edited by Dorothy Bass

What's So Amazing about Grace? by Philip Yancey

Dare to Be Uncommon, Quiet Strength, and the Mentor Leader by Tony Dungy

Trusting in God When Times Are Tough by Ed Hindson

Unstuck: Out of Your Cave and into Your Call by Mark Jobe

CHAPTER 6

Emerging Small Batch Communities and Their Values

Missional communities have clarity and focus around their common life and a clear ministry for the people they serve. They have gone through a process of praying, discerning, and beginning to go out to meet. They've done the hard work of getting to know their neighbors, and they are really building community out in the world with these different groups. They are focused. In other words, they're not doing this plus five other things. They're going to do this. This is what they do, and they have a common life around prayer, scripture reading, and worship that goes along with that.

What are the basic characteristics of a small batch missional community? What are the essentials? First, a few individuals are sent out of their church to create a missional community. They immerse themselves in their local neighborhood and find partners there. They create their own structures based on the type of community they are creating, leaving behind the structures and burdens of the sending church. They spend their whole ministry outside of the sending church. They grow their ministry out of the organic life shared with community members. Evangelism is exemplified, not taught. Formation is explored. Membership follows service.

There are different kinds of missional communities that a sending church can co-create with its neighbors. We have a tendency to categorize these quickly. We want to be able to put some framework and model around them. The church, its leaders, and its members will always want to create a new procrustean bed. We must resist this temptation. The evangelical churches have been experimenting with these small batch communities for over twenty years and have been somewhat successful. However, the issues they have center around the fact that they have programmed them. We need to learn from our evangelical brothers and sisters, by all means. They have a variety of books that are listed in the back. However, we must be careful not to narrowly categorize these efforts. We must, as a church, open ourselves up to the great variety of cultural expressions of Christian community as we can possibly imagine.

I want to tease out some terms that we've used in the past and to think clearly about different kinds of missional communities that are being imagined. While the Episcopal Church has largely abandoned college campus ministry over the last two decades, it is time to reengage. This is one of the prime mission contexts for the future church. However, mission on college campuses will not look like blown-up youth ministry for college kids. Instead the future of campus missions will look like a disbursement model mission. No longer will undergrad and graduate co-eds find their way to a campus center where the one campus missioner works.

Instead the campus mission, like the networked church, will have nodes of connection throughout the campus. A college campus mission at a tier-one school might actually start college missions on local community college campuses as well. The future church no longer sees campus mission as a secondary isolated ministry for kids, but as a primary mission site where the gospel is shared throughout the campus community.

At the Episcopal campus ministries that remain, peer ministry was and still is largely used as the dominant model. An insular model with one clergy leader running program limits the distribution of the ministry because it centers itself on the place and person of a campus missioner. The distributed college campus mission will be aided by a move away from this insular and centralized ministry, to a student leadership team aimed outward. The Reverend Joe Chambers at Rockwell House at Washington University in St. Louis changed over to this new model several years ago. The Reverend Mike Angell from the Episcopal Church Office supports campus and young adult ministries, and he believes the outward-facing, team-led campus mission is beginning to catch on and spread. Young adults on college campuses are interested in creating real communities bound together by relationships and with dispersed mission across the campus.

We will see house churches in urban, suburban, and even rural areas. Some of these will be connected to the larger church community as mentioned above. However, many more will be stand-alone. You may have one missioner priest with a team of lay leaders overseeing twenty or more of these small communities.[83] The Barna Group has been predicting this since the 1990s, and I have been teaching and talking about this for over two decades. Yet the Episcopal Church has had difficulty engaging this model because we have been primarily stuck in a centralized churchy model.

We will have cyber churches.[84] Some people have taken cyber church to mean a SimCity[85] type environment where people go to church online. People have created online gaming-type congregations similar to the Sims. The cyber church of tomorrow will be a church community that gathers online and shares information and news but does not have a permanent place. The cyber church of the future will use the distributive model of ministry to connect nodes of ministry in space and time throughout the community. It will be a church that uses different public spaces for worship, teaching, and Bible study. It will adopt other service ministry sites for its outreach. The primary connection point for members will be the smartphone, and they will be connected through the Internet to their brothers and sisters, sharing prayers, thoughts, and experiences. They will find out the community schedule and go to the coffee shop for a Bible study, meet in a park for prayer and meditation, and work at a local clinic serving the poor and those in need.

Another kind of community in the future church is described by the Barna Group as an event church. "Frustrated with politics and structures in the standard church, many will participate infrequently in worship events in public places."[86] I think we are going to have communities pop up for limited times around special events or other gatherings. I think we might see communities pop up during the Daytona 500 or in the parking lots on Sunday mornings during tailgate season at the local NFL game or Saturdays on college game day. We already see this on Easter in parks and on other special days. But I think congregations engaged in a disbursement model will be looking for ways to send missionaries, pastors, and priests out to be present where people are. Flash mob Eucharist[87] and the presence of the church in the midst of the modern-day public square are mission opportunities of the future.

Service communities will be another kind of church that emerges strongly in the next ten years.[88] These will be communities that rise up around particular ministries. We see this already occurring where there is an outreach to the poor or those in need following a disaster. Communities spring up. People choose to worship with those they are serving. A great example is the outreach of Trinity Parish in Houston, which grew up around ministry to the homeless. Today it is called Lord of the Streets. They started serving Eucharist following Sunday morning breakfast. What first started as something that was done for the homeless is now something that is done with the homeless and working poor in Houston. People choose to make this early morning service the service they attend. The community does its own Bible study, and it is creating a pastoral care ministry and becoming a mix of people of every ethnicity and social stratum who choose to work together. I know of similar communities in Atlanta and Los Angeles.

The monastic type community will spring up as a revitalized part of the church's mission.[89] In the Episcopal Church, we already have a service corps whose chief hallmark is living in community together (http://episcopalservicecorps.org). Focused on a ministry of service, they live in community with daily prayer and Bible study. They have a chaplain who mentors and watches over the community life.[90] Still others are simply communities that share a common rule of life. The Missional Wisdom Foundation operates a network of distributed but connected new monastic communities in North Texas (missionalwisdom.com). Small groups of individuals choose to live together under one roof and one rule of life. They participate in the community. We are even now talking about how these same models might be adapted for people in their senior years who would like to live with others.

Many individuals will find community life by participating in what Barna calls "dialogue forums."[91] These will be where people gather in small groups to talk about spirituality or discipleship or read the Bible. This will take place in people's homes, coffee shops, condominium community spaces, and pubs. Many Episcopal churches have dipped their toe into this well over the last two decades, beginning with "Theology on Tap." Diocese of Texas churches joined churches across the country in 2003 in offering conversation over beer and food at a local pub. These were extensions of existing congregations. Every church will need to be doing this kind of disbursed mission in the future. Individuals are going to look for spiritual opportunities closer to home or their workplaces, and such communities will be an important way in which community life is lived out outside of the parish. It literally creates new doors into the community. Many people who are not attached to a community will find it much easier to be invited and to connect to communities like this. This is going to grow and become an essential ingredient of regular community life.

The compassion cluster is a short-term community located around a particular effort.[92] These will grow up in the midst of tent cities that are doing work around a particular crisis. Along the Gulf Coast, we see these pop up after hurricanes. People come from all over and participate in a community of faith that springs up like the temporary towns, which house food, volunteer support, shelter, and showers for those being served and those serving. We also saw this happen in the midst of those who went to help clean up and rebuild after devastating wildfires in Bastrop, Texas. During the Occupy Wall Street movement in New York, clergy went in and preached and celebrated the Eucharist amongst the protesters. As we become more aware of events such as these, people engaged in them will bring both their desire for community and worship with them. The Episcopal churches in any given area of the United States need to be aware that such compassion clusters are opportunities to reach out, serve, and get to know others.

Small groups and prayer shelters will continue to multiply.[93] Some of these are around reading books together. Others were kaffee klatsches that now have developed a life of praying together. The individuals in these small communities may belong to other organizations, or they may not be affiliated with any. They are primarily based upon friendship models. Throughout the 1970s and 1980s, Episcopal Cursillo Reunion groups served as a way to organize a growing popularity of this kind of mission. They were essential in the growth that was seen during those years for many communities. They began to fizzle out for the same reason as do many ministries. They became institutionalized. Such groups, like the discussion groups, have an important potential of undergirding a distributive missionary system.

Another community that will be part of the distributed autopoietic mission strategy is the marketplace ministry.[94] I remember that we actually stopped this from happening in our diocese. We had several clergy who had begun to provide pastoral care for workers at a local chicken-processing center. At the time I don't think we could wrap our minds around why this had value. There are still a number of companies who have chaplains on staff to help take care of their workers. I actually believe that these corporate chaplains are not long for the world. The economic situation has caused the funds for such excesses to dry up, and as an ancillary part of the corporation, such services are being dropped. Hospital chaplains are also going by the wayside as the cost of health care and the margin for financial success are growing slim.

We must engage in this ministry. These places are still sites for ministry. We need to send lay and ordained people out to be with people in the places where they live and work. The church must recognize that we still have a mission into these marketplaces, hospitals, and retirement communities, even if we do not own them or are paid to do them. These are the many and varied places where the people are and God is. Therefore it is imperative for us to make this an important part of our distributive mission focus.

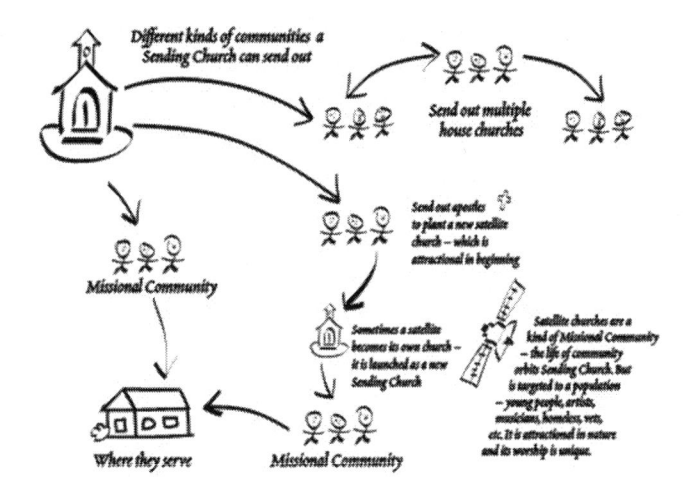

This is, of course, not meant to be a complete list of the future church's missional communities. There will be more kinds of Christian communities created by future missionaries that we cannot even imagine today but will be intimately tied to future cultural contexts.

So imagine all kinds of different ministries. The sending church sends people out in the world to create these new communities, and this is not something that is new to the church. It is new to us within the last seventy years, but it is not a new thing, and there are even blips of it if we look at the 1940s, 1950s, and 1960s in Houston as people sent out what today we would call "missional communities." Remember, during Christianity's most prolific time of expansion, the small batch, local, organic, and sustainable missional community was the order of the day.

Bob Johansen and the folks at the Institute for the Future (IFTF) believe we can see artifacts of the future in our society today.[95] We can see artifacts of our present future church too. What we do with this information will determine our future. In 2008, Johansen sat down with leaders of endowed parishes to discuss what the future Episcopal Church might look like. Johansen challenged the group to see the bits and pieces of artifacts from the surrounding culture as "provocative moments." He questioned, "Can we sift through the flotsam and jetsam of the future that even now is washing up upon our shores as we make our way through the perilous waves undaunted?"[96] Today we are more than years into those pregnant ideas, having only begun to take our first steps.

If we are going to speak about church communities, we need to look at what is happening in the context around us. If we are going to speak about whom we raise up as missionaries, we look at how people are trained today. If we are to speak about stewardship, we need to look at how people use, spend, and network money. If we are going to talk about service and outreach, we need to look at how people are doing this today. In each scenario we are able to perceive the gap between where we are today and where the future lies. When we see the gap, we are able then to move into it and begin to create the future church. So I am constantly looking for images and examples of what is happening in the world around the nature of community and how that might help us to understand better how to do the work of forming community.

I was recently invited to speak to a group of Methodists interested in the future of denominationalism and specifically the Methodist tradition. In a beautiful moment of synchronicity, blind luck, stupendous grace, and Holy Spirit work, I was introduced to two amazing students from Harvard, Angie Thurston and Casper ter Kuile. Thurston is interested in deepening community and understanding how millennials and the nones (as they are currently called), who are finding themselves disaffiliated from mainline religion as they are finding their spiritual way in the world. She is currently doing work with a company in Colorado on values.

ter Kuile is heading into parish ministry, the co-founder of UK Youth Climate Coalition and Campaign Bootcamp. Full of energy, he too is interested in exploring questions and trends in the emerging culture. Thanks to the help of the Crestwood Foundation, they were able to study cultural trends in community making.[97] Both Thurston and ter Kuile claim they have been and are unaffiliated. I will tell you that my experience of these two is really powerfully grounded individuals on the pilgrimage of a lifetime. They certainly connected with me and this work around small batch communities.

Over two years they studied the following groups: The Dinner Party, Good People Dinners, deliberateLIFE, The Civil Conversations Project from On Being, HONY For The Holidays, Mend, CrossFit, November Project, Tough Mudder, Spartan Race, StickK, No Meat Athlete, SoulCycle, Pure Barre, Brooklyn Boulders, Zumba, Redisco, Morning Gloryville, CTZNWELL, The Feast, Junto, Off the Mat, Into the World, Relational Center, The Catalyst Collective, US Department of Arts and Culture, The Harry Potter Alliance, Thread, The Moth, Couchsurfing, StoryCorps, Millennial Trains Project, Mycelium, Wisdom Hackers, Open Master's, The Unreasonable Institute, Live in the Grey, The Bold Academy, Coach.me, Kindly App, 7 Cups of Tea, Lantern, ImpactHUB, Juniper Path, Headspace, Global Spiritual Life at NYU, Search Inside Yourself Leadership Institute, Camp Grounded, Awesomeness Fest, Summit Series, TheGlint, Groupmuse, Artisan's Asylum, The Go Game, Mousai, Movies and Meaning, The Sanctuaries, Bodhi Spiritual Center, and Sunday Assembly.[98]

As I have begun this conversation, I constantly hear, "Millennials don't join things." This phrase is typically uttered by an older person who is bemoaning the fact that his or her congregation is not able to hold on to younger people. Basically that phrase has come to mean, "It is their fault they don't like us." It is a way of projecting our fear about our own future communities and removing responsibility from ourselves. It is a way to throw in the towel rather than change things.

The reality is, as you look across the electronic universe and this long list of organizations, what you see is that actually people are joining things. They just aren't interested in much of what we are doing and much of what we call church. There are over six thousand CrossFits, and over two hundred thousand people took part in their annual games in 2015.

I am not going to give all their findings here, because you really need to read the report to understand the culture created by these varying organizations. Thurston and ter Kuile studied and mapped out the groups' "ancestry, sibling projects, and cousins in corporate America."[99] The ethos they found across all of these organizations was a mutually shared desire by the participants for "community, personal transformation, social transformation, purpose finding, creativity, and accountability."[100]

Some other insights that were important begin with careful thought from leaders. In each case the leaders saw a need in the community and decided to do something. This is key. To start a new community, leaders have to have a vision and the courage to begin. The second insight is that a lot of these tend to be working with very affluent, urban, and educated people. And these people are the vast majority of the unaffiliated.[101] However, and most importantly, groups like the Sanctuaries and the US Department of Arts and Culture (not a government organization) are breaking open models and building diverse communities of mutuality. Certainly the groups mentioned in this book are having some success across social, cultural, and race divides.

In visiting with them over breakfast, they are clear they don't think they have found a magic bullet for mission. Yet they remain curious about how the people who participate in these groups experience transcendence. Today Thurston and ter Kuile are working on the next phase of their project and releasing more data. Their work is very exciting and points to important insights about patterns we may wish to adapt as we create our own smaller communities.

I think what is important in their work is that these groups are reflecting the best pieces of Christian community in their lives and culture. I would point out that these categories are very much in line with traditional Anglican mission. Values of community, personal transformation, social transformation, purpose-finding, creativity, and accountability are present in the best of Christian community. The old way of thinking about mission is to think about worship style or church-building. The new mission-oriented leaders will be thinking more about people, community, and context-making.

One of my favorite groups they studied was the Sanctuaries (http://thesanctuaries.org). They state that their purpose is, "We're empowering creative people of diverse backgrounds to claim their own spiritual voice, express themselves artistically, and collaborate with others to promote social change."[102] They write,

> We exist. We live in a diverse yet segregated city. Our community is changing that. We're bringing creative and soulful people together to build community, not just another crowd. Our members keep it real, without all the drama and judgment. We believe that every story matters. And that in order to get the most out of life, we have to invest in our creative and spiritual lives.
>
> We're better together. It's that simple.

What We're About

Whether we're performing an original song at one of our Soul Slams or painting a mural with a friend, everything we do involves:

- Creativity: Be real. Express yourself.
- Spirituality: Focus on what matters most.
- Justice: Create a world that works for all of us.

1. Check us out. The best way to see what we're about is to come to one of our upcoming events (below).
2. Be our guest. Afterward we'll invite you to our member-led gatherings to meet other folks and hang out.
3. Make it official. If it's a good fit, you can become a member to get the most out of our community.[103]

We have so become accustomed to doing worship as our chief and primary form of evangelism that we have forgotten that Christian community can happen around all kinds of creative possibilities and break down all social boundaries. At its best, it has done this, and from these rich communal experiences flows belonging and table fellowship.

Dispatches from the Front: The Slate Project

The Reverend Sara Shisler Goff is the gifted convener of the Slate Project (TSP), a missional community that models multidimensional engagement. You can take your online pilgrimage to TSP here, http://www.slateproject.org. *This is their story.*

TSP is a new kind of Christian community that gathers both online and face-to-face in Baltimore, Maryland. We are committed to following the way of Jesus together into our local and digital neighborhoods and discerning as a community how to be the church in the twenty-first century. We describe ourselves as rooted in the ancient, the arts, and the commitment to social justice action. Our mission is to reimagine what the church can be by focusing on the core of Christian faith, the call to love God with all our heart, soul, mind, and strength and to love our neighbor as ourselves.

How It Began

In 2013, The Reverends Jason Chesnut, Jennifer DiFrancesco, and Sara Shisler Goff were all working in separate parishes in separate denominations, and yet they were all experiencing similar frustrations in their ministries. They experienced a similar longing to do something new. Goff would say, "It would be more accurate to say that God was already doing something new and we were longing to join in."

Jason had been hired by the Delaware Maryland Synod of the ELCA to be the mission developer for Baltimore. Jennifer and Sara had both been working at parishes in Baltimore for several years and knew each other from joint ministry endeavors. Over a serendipitous bread bowl of Maryland crab dip, the three of them shared their longings and their questions. They imagined together:

> What if we could go back, like way back? Like back to the beginning back. Back to when there was no church. Back to when there was no Christianity. Back to when there were followers of this guy named Jesus, who believed he was the Son of God and after his death they became followers of the Way. What if we could spend some time sifting through all that has happened since then? Some of it has been good, but some of it has been ... not so good. Some if it has been downright awful. We decided to go ahead and call the awful stuff what it is, crap. Christianity has a lot of crap. The crap is in all those places where Christianity and Christians have failed to incarnate the liberative power of the gospel and instead have perpetuated oppression, violence, and a bunch of other evils.

They felt it was important for the church going forward to name those times and places where Christianity has fallen short and to repent of the evil that still enslaves us. They had a holy vision and clarity. They knew the mission challenge was, for the most part, many Americans today see Christians as judgmental, hypocritical, and irrelevant.

They decided that part of what they wanted to do was to name the crap and then practice the ancient Christian rituals of confession, repentance, and reconciliation, to turn back toward God and recommit to following Jesus along the way. This was a bold vision forward, filled with accountability and some very real, ancient Christian practice. They had a sense of reestablishing the very real holy work of mission.

The more they talked, the more excited they became. They pondered, prayed, and began to dream. They wondered together,

> What if we could claim the good in our Christian traditions and leave the rest? Then we could take that good stuff and reimagine how to live out our Christian faith in the present day! We could reimagine how to live the Way of the followers of Jesus in our own postmodern world. We each had a very strong conviction that this way of Jesus can only be discerned and practiced together in community.

A friend of Jason's had suggested the "Slate Project," like "a blank slate." That worked for Jenn and Sara; thus the Slate Project was born.

They are very clear about their purpose and work. They maintain their clarity and mission by having clear expectations of their community and shared life. They do the following:

- Feed each other, both physically and spiritually, by sharing a weekly meal together and practicing the spiritual disciplines of sharing story, prayer, service, and study
- Break down barriers that keep people apart, particularly at the intersections of differences such as race, class, age, socioeconomic status, ethnicity, sexual orientation, education, and life experience
- Create a place of belonging where people are welcome to bring their entire selves, take what they need, and offer what they have to give
- Practice repentance, confession, and reconciliation in our individual and communal relationships
- Develop and maintain strong relationships grounded in God
- Reclaim the Bible as a story worth telling
- Partner with others in rebuilding our neighborhoods to be places where all people can flourish

TSP community gathers both online and face-to-face in Baltimore. Their weekly face-to-face worship experience happens on Monday nights with a dinner liturgy we call #BreakingBread. Everyone is invited to participate in transforming our borrowed space from a parish hall (graciously offered by the Episcopal Cathedral of the Incarnation and the Diocese of Maryland) into an intimate dinner setting for thirty or so people. They gather in darkness with song and a word of welcome before lighting candles and moving into a circle to share the bread. Conversation and fellowship happen over dinner, and then someone from the community leads a time of teaching and reflection before we close with prayer and the cup.

Their weekly online gathering is a Twitter chat called #SlateSpeak, where people from all over the world join in at 9:00 p.m. (EST) for an hour of theological conversation. They pray, introduce themselves, and dive right in to the evening's topic, usually related to the week's national or global events and related to the designated theme we are currently exploring.

They usually combine their themes together in a series related to the church calendar. For example, for Lent in 2015, they brought back the photo-a-day challenge they piloted in 2014 (#reLent) and framed it by focusing each week on a different Christology:

- Week 1—The Black Christ
- Week 2—The Poor Christ
- Week 3—The Queer Christ
- Week 4—The Feminist Christ
- Week 5—The Disabled Christ
- Week 6—The Nonviolent Christ

Each week they invited a different person from the community with a particular interest or connection that Christology to teach during #BreakingBread about his or her experience of this particular way of understanding Christ. They also filmed that person in a short video spot discussing that week's Christology and posted it to their YouTube page. The daily digital content would also focus on that week's Christological theme. Their digital content includes the memes they create and post on social media, the blog posts they write, and any other videos or podcasts they create.

Throughout the last three years, they have experimented with various digital media series. #BibleUnplugged, #AdventUs #YoureWelcomeWednesdays, [Throwback]Thursdays, Mean Christian Tweets, and #JesusCoffeeFridays are just a few examples. If they gain traction, they keep going. If they do not garner much excitement (get shared, liked, commented on, and so forth), they stop and try something else.

They are committed to providing ways for people to engage with the community online in some way at least once a day. They currently offer two face-to-face gatherings during the week. In addition to #BreakingBread, they have a weekly Bible study called #WakeUpWordUp on Wednesday mornings at 7:30 a.m. Since it is so early, they meet at a local coffee shop so there is plenty of caffeine available, and as co-pastor Jason says, "We try really hard for it not to suck." This means facilitating engagement with the text rather than providing information to be consumed. They say they take the Bible seriously, not literally. They do not work to make the Bible relevant for people's lives. They introduce without apology the awesome and crazy stories the Bible contains. Often that is enough to get others hooked.

Initially they were surprised by the kind of people who were engaging with TSP. In the very beginning their target audience was the unchurched, the dechurched, and the nones. What was surprising was that they started to attract people who were involved in other church communities, often in leadership roles, but needed something more. They discovered that people in ministry needed a place where they could be fed instead of doing all the feeding. They needed a place to share their frustrations and disappointments with the church. They needed a place where change was part of the ethos. The Slate team ended up attracting a lot of people like themselves. Perhaps that should not have been surprising. They did get some non-church folks, which was awesome. And they got a good number of folks who are food and/or housing insecure. People came for the meal and stayed for the community.

Overall TSP is made up of people committed to figuring out together what it means to be a Christian community in the twenty-first century. They are constantly asking ourselves, "What if we had a blank slate for being the church?" This helps them to discern what is really at the heart of what it means to be the church: what they need to hold on to and carry into the future and what they can release. Some typical ways of doing church are not necessary for their context, so they can let them go.

For example at this time, they do not need a building, so they do not have one. They do not have membership requirements because they want to offer a broad range of ways to engage with the Slate community and not focus on who is in and who is out. They are supported by three denominations, but they do not focus on denominational identity. They feel they can do more focusing on common mission and what they can do together as Christians from various traditions rather than separating themselves denominationally. Plus they are learning about each other's traditions. And their comfort with ecumenical diversity is serving them well as they move toward doing more interfaith collaboration and partnering with others in the city of Baltimore.

The main mission, the core reason TSP continues to exist, is to be a place where people can practice being in loving relationships with one another. They have all had experiences with other people in the church that have not felt grounded in love. This is to be expected because they are human. But it is upsetting because they desire the church to be what it says it is, a place of love. The Slate members remind us that we need to remember that love also includes confessing when we are wrong, forgiving when we are hurt, reconciling and healing when we are broken, and doing it all over again.

The question that Slate is asking is, "How do we as Christians recenter ourselves in the heart of what it means to be the church?" They would argue this means recognizing themselves as communities of individuals bonded together by and in the Holy Spirit and recommitting to loving each other and all of creation with the love of God that is within us.

In some ways, Slate is not doing anything new. Every church community can do what they have done by asking themselves, "What if we had a blank slate?" Essentially this is saying, "These relationships that make up the church, universally and particularly, are important enough to us that, rather than walk away, we, in a sense, want to start over. Let's recommit. Let's remember why we love each other in the first place. We are children of God. We love because God first loves us. Now let's talk about how we can do this better. In other words, how we can be in relationships that we can all agree are grounded in love?"

What They Learned

They have learned that the intention to do things differently will not prevent them from falling back into old habits. From the very beginning, Jenn, Jason, and Sara wanted TSP to be the co-creation of the entire community, not just the three of them. They have had to continually remind themselves to let go and wait: wait for the right time, wait for the right people, and wait for the Holy Spirit. There is always something they could be doing. Like so many of us, they know how to do church. They can do church in their sleep. But doing church just to do it isn't enough. In fact that is part of the problem. They have to be the church. And that takes another whole level of intentionality and commitment. It is also what makes it possible.

Creating a new community is a very long process. There is no way that it can be done in two or three years, the time frame most denominations give their church planters and mission developers to figure out how they are going to be sustainable. There are two problems with this. First, it is not nearly enough time. According to the Center for Progressive Renewal, forming a new community takes at least ten years.

Second, the whole idea of sustainability sounds more and more like coded language for "self-perpetuating," which is where the institutional church is stuck. Church communities should last as long as they are meant to last, meaning as long as they serve their mission/purpose and as long as there are committed people to do the work of being community. Without those things, the community has already ceased to exist. It is just on life support. The church has forgotten that we do not need to be afraid of death. We are all called to be a resurrection people. But we cannot actually get to the resurrection without the death. This is what TSP is trying to remember.

As long as there are people committed to TSP's mission, it will exist. Of course we are committed and will work hard to keep it going, but the shift in focus from anxiously trying to stay alive to graciously continuing to live out the faith makes all the difference. Everything has a season. Every created thing has a life and a death. They must embrace the full cycle of life and death and see the blessings in each part.

What They Might Do Differently

Sara felt the longing in her soul to take the leap of faith and go all in with TSP for a long time before she actually did it. Jason has been the full-time Lutheran mission developer for Baltimore since TSP began. Jenn and Sara have always had paying jobs at other churches and co-pastored TSP at the same time but with no compensation. That will change for Sara in January 2016 when the Episcopal Diocese of Maryland will start to compensate her (part time) for her work with Slate. Their next goal is to bring Jenn on part time as well.

Many people cannot wrap their head around why one church would need three pastors. First of all, they are the only staff, and none of their work is siloed. Each one does a bit of everything, and they work together on quite a lot. There is no one pastor who can be all things to all people. The three of them cannot be all things to all people, but together they sure can cover a lot more territory. And for them, the act of pastoring together has been much healthier and more fulfilling than other hierarchical models they have experienced. Sara writes,

I have found it much easier to invite others into a shared leadership model that already exists amongst the pastors, than attempting to invite shared leadership under a hierarchical model. Shared leadership provides for more creativity, accountability, support—and it's a hell of a lot more fun. I think two of the biggest reasons clergy stop doing church planting is because they burn out (trying to do all the work by themselves) and because the work is so isolating (doing all the work by themselves.) Remember, Jesus sent his disciples out two by two. If two is good, three is better.

Questions

1. Bishop Doyle urges us to resist the temptation to categorize small batch communities too quickly, but he also suggests they share a few common values. How do you reconcile this tension? What do you see as the core values around which the many and diverse expressions of Christian community will self-organize in the future?
2. The work of Angie Thurston and Casper ter Kuile debunks the myth that "millennials don't join things." Are millennials currently joining your congregation? How might your community need to change to pique the interest of millennials?
3. Bishop Doyle says TSP is ecumenical (supported by three denominations) and yet does "not focus on denominational identity." Do you believe that denominations have a role to play in the future church? Can a Christian community remain faithful to her denomination without focusing on it?
4. Think of the Christian community you attend. If you had a blank slate for being the church, what aspects of your community would you hold on to? What would you want to release?

Recommendations for Further Reading

Community: The Structure of Belonging by Peter Block

Holy Currencies: 6 Blessings for Sustainable Missional Ministries by Eric H. F. Law

Leaders Make the Future: Ten New Leadership Skills for an Uncertain World by Bob Johansen

Behavioral Covenants in Congregations: A Handbook for Honoring Differences by Gilbert R. Rendle

Rising Strong: The Reckoning. The Rumble. The Revolution by Brene Brown

Chapter 7

A Budding Missiology

Episcopal churches are being called to create a new (ancient) kind of community. This community will be about connection, belonging, loving, and purposeful work/ministry. All congregations are hardwired for a particular kind of community. Our missiology, our theology of mission, has greatly affected the nature of who our congregations are as attractional communities. As we explore the deeper meaning of what it means to be a sending church with missional communities, we will need to understand that we are talking about a different kind of missiology.

The deep difference between attractional communities and the missional communities is an essential piece to doing the work well. I want to be clear, as we explore these differences, I give no value to one or the other. One is not wrong, and one is not right. As we have already said, both models of church are needed as we lean into the new missionary age. Furthermore, if we aren't clear about what the model of ministry we are using in existing congregations, if we don't name clearly the difference in evangelism, we will likely simply re-create smaller attractional communities rather than multiplying our efforts. What would be tragic is if we replicated and multiplied the problems existing in our churches today into the church of tomorrow.

Attractional Church Missiology

So let us think a bit about the missiology of our attractional communities. People are drawn to them, and most of the ministries that take place there are, in fact, centered on the sustenance of the community.

So in attractional churches, people do some outreach and service work, but most of the ministries are ministries focused on worship or discipleship in the community. Proportionately, ministry in church is about the ministry of church. This means that clergy have a lot of power, worship is the key ingredient (sometimes the only), and the majority of the money goes to support the congregation with only a fraction going outside to affect health in the community neighborhood.

Therefore these attractional communities have a particular nature. They have a kind of authenticity.[104] The community itself has an authentic nature or quality. They are old, young, and filled with families. Their worship is beautiful and complex with incense, bells, and wonderful vestments. Or their worship is simple with contemporary music and filled with multimedia images and sound. The community may be small or large. It may have programs for all kinds of interests, or it may have one Bible study.

Think for a moment about the words you would use in describing your church community. You probably go to a wonderful attractional church. It is authentically unique and special. Here is the important thing to understand: in an attractional community, the person who comes through the front door looks at the authenticity of the community and chooses whether this community is for him or her. He or she chooses to become part of the community; consequently he or she chooses to fit into the community.

These authentic communities are less focused on the authenticity of the individual, so they tend to be very monocultural. People are attracted by like-mindedness and comfort with the socioeconomic, ethnic, and cultural definitions present in the community. These congregations have to labor hard to break free of this imposed like-mindedness, and it is very difficult. In fact it is easier to start a new congregation with another set of cultural identifying characteristics than it is to transform an existing one.

The first characteristic of the attractional missiology is that the community is invested in enculturation into the community. We might say that the discipleship model is to have the new member become authentically a disciple of the community.

The second missiological characteristic is rooted in the caretaking of the community's authenticity, self-compassion. The attractional community is compassionate primarily to its own identity. The community works diligently to say clearly who they are and what they stand for and to make a case that these are the values of the community and community members. This inculcates in the community a concern for itself and sympathy for the communal work. People within the community and those who are new come to understand and care for the life of the community as a whole.

A healthy attractional community defends itself over shifts that threaten its authentic identity. It has an idea about itself, works to create better communication, and passes on its identity through those who are sympathetic to its cause and nature. Discipleship is key in this model, and it is frequently the only thing that is important. The community wants to build a group (large or small) of individuals who are devoted to the community and will caretake and tend its life.

The attractional church builds a resilient spirit as a missiological principle by taking charge of its life and being self-sustaining. It builds systems internally to support its life and work. Structure, volunteers, and staff are the skeletal infrastructure of this community. It is not particularly flexible, though it may use new cultural tools to accomplish the old-time, worn characteristics of the community. The attractional church's resiliency is evident in the fact that, despite civil wars, cultural wars, changing economic circumstances, movements of the Holy Spirit, and reformations, the attractional church remains intact as the primary form of Christian community today.

The attractional community's missiology is one of gratitude and joy. Celebrations are communal within the life of the community itself. Its primary feasts are the feasts of its contextual calendar. It gives thanks for the impact the community has had on the individuals. Within the attractional community, there is a sense that we give thanks for its life and ministry. We give thanks for the community members' presence there. We mark the life of the community members as part of the wider life of the community. There may be birthday and anniversary prayers, but the great thanksgivings are for the high holy days, the martyrs and saints of the congregation. The sacraments are key in this life of gratitude and joy. These and the calendar days that mark their usage protect the community members from the world outside itself.

The attractional community works in a particular way as we have described. We trust the model. It has a way of being that those who examine it can intuit. For instance, we can tell budget size by average Sunday attendance. We can describe its life if we know a few things about it. We are easily able to understand the work of the people there without a lot of information.

The attractional community is sure of its place within the wider Christian community and the wider culture. Despite recent concerns over the attractional church's future, the reality is that those concerns arise out of the closing of smaller attractional churches or the financial difficulties of others. In truth, the attractional community's future is certain, healthy, and viable.

The missiological quality of trust and assurance are present for the members of the attractional community. Those who enter know and understand that the community is there for them. As it works out its life, it will be around for a long time to come. The member who takes on the qualities of the community and invests in its life can count on the community being there for them in good times and bad. The community will be there to baptize their children and grandchildren and to bury them when the time comes.

Creativity is an essential part of the attractional community's healthy missiology. It has to be creative, constantly adapting to the culture shifts and forces around it. How we do formation, communication, banking, leadership, and new starts are all examples of how the attractional community over the years has adapted. Creativity is typically slow in the attractional community as change, while it does come, comes at a comfortable pace that does not disturb community life too much.

Play, rest, and the cultivation of calm and stillness are essential ingredients to the attractional community's missiology. The community is the primary place, or at least aims to be the primary place of rest, calm, and stillness away from the rest of the world. Consequently many spaces are used for prayer and Sabbath-keeping. The play of life within the community centers around how it works, celebrates, and serves others.

As an authentic Christian community, regardless of what kind, the work and life of the community is meaningful. The missiology of the community is to do meaningful work within the wider culture in which it finds itself. It is about providing meaningful work for those who tend and care for it. Performing altar guild and lay reading, serving at the altar, teaching Sunday School, helping with the youth ministry, welcoming new people, and serving the poor are spiritual exercises. Each piece of work is meaningful within the community for those who do the work and is treasured as an offering by God as gift.

Laughter, song, and the dance of liturgy are essential ingredients within the community. The ritual within the community transforms the difficult times, and the individual finds he or she is not alone. They are part of a family with its own rhythm and beat. The sharing of life and the sacred music of the community are not only part of its authenticity. They are part of the transformative medicine for the sin-sick soul. The great song of Miriam is a reminder and hallmark of the community's nature to dance and sing. Exodus 15.20ff says, "Then the prophet Miriam, Aaron's sister, took a tambourine in her hand; and all the women went out after her with tambourines and with dancing. And Miriam sang to them: 'Sing to the Lord, for he has triumphed gloriously …'" The community and its faith are protected, they are upheld, and their laughter, song, and dance is an outward expression of their inner belonging to the greater whole.

Sending Community Missiology

The missiology of the sending congregation with its missional communities has the same qualities of authenticity, self-compassion, and so forth. However, where the attractional community is always focused upon the communal life and the individual's place within it, the missional community is focused upon the individual and their community context. It is an outward-oriented missiology interested in the life lived in the world. Where the attractional church is interested in Christ found in the community of the church, the sending church and missional community is interested in finding Christ in the community of the world.

So the missional community sees the missiological value of authenticity as primarily being focused upon the individual it meets outside the Church. It is invested in the diversity of people wherein is found Christ. They believe that God is out in the world in all kinds of places, in the midst of all kinds of communities, and within all kinds of human beings.

Those who leave the confines of the church go out into the world to find the unique expression of Christ in the unique individuals of the neighborhood. They cultivate authenticity by being open to the people they meet. Those who go out do so without a desire to transform people, but rather to be transformed by the people they meet. They go out authentically Christian with a desire to serve, live, and be with those they find. They may pray, "Lord show yourself in the people I meet and serve." I believe the key missiological principle here is that God is authentically in the world and those apostles who go out must lose their church life in order to find God.

Jesus went out into the crowds. He went to the people. He sailed and walked where they sailed and walked. He entered their homes and places of work. He met them and allowed them to be who they were. Together they were transformed into a new blossoming community of God. Casting out demons, forgiving sin, healing the sick, and sharing the Word he had been given, Jesus became part of the community in the world. He was not simply in the world, but as he was in the world, he cared and cared for the things they cared about. Remember he saw them as sheep without a shepherd and was moved in his gut. He had compassion for them. He worked with those he found out in the world, and together they worked to make the world better. He joined together with a band of brothers and sisters. He sent them as apostles. They, in turn, went out, and upon their return they said to him,

"You would not believe what happened. People were made well, the devil fell down before us, and mighty works were done."

Self-compassion is present in the sending community missiology. Letting go of the ideas around what community is supposed to look like, the apostle allows the shape of the community to form around those concerns that reside in the community. Those who go out are freed from the concerns of economies of scale and the requirement to maintain buildings and structures, even egos. They go out and ask: What is the community's need for compassion? How can the community and I care for itself? What are the needs here, and how do we care for one another in this place?

An important way that self-compassion is present is that the apostles who go out are not concerned with replicating the community from which they were sent. They understand that attempting some perfect idea of a community from the past is to cut off the authenticity and ability to listen to the people in the world. They go out with a sense of discovery, not to recreate their idea about community but to find a community awaiting them, a community already filled with God and the Holy Spirit.

The apostles, as they go out, will cultivate a resilient spirit. They will do this by not taking with them the huge amounts of baggage that comes with the attractional church. Jesus sends people out with very little. He sends them out without bag, sandals, or tunic (Luke 9:3). The apostles are sent out, completely dependent upon the community to which they go. Resilience is found in that they are not burdened by structure, ideas, or mandates. They go instead with a pliable spirit.

At its best the attractional church naturally uses power, structures, and authority in healthy ways to build strength and resilience. The dark side of the attractional church is when it uses these things to control and protect. Small batch communities are also imperfect; they have a shadow side. They have difficulty in that they, as a new and idealized form of church, may not find value in the context of life and ministry lived in connection to a wider rule of life. They may also believe they are the only future.

Policy rarely is the mother of creativity and the Holy Spirit. Though the attractional church can, like all institutions, create a numbing process by believing that all of the maintenance that must be done is essential to gospel mission. In the sending churches, they do maintenance, and they have policies, but the apostles are freed to invest in work that is less structured and less controlled by the needs of the wider organization. While people in a larger organization can feel powerless within the system, in the missional community, people are empowered to do the work. The work of the baptized is preaching, teaching, leading worship, and pastoring the community. By doing work that the Holy Spirit is giving people to do, they are enlivened for the ministry and not weakened by its drain. My wife says, regarding Facebook, "If you are not having fun, you are doing it wrong." I think this is a good mantra for sorting out how missional community work cultivates a resilient spirit. Having fun and playing in the fields of the Lord's harvest is a key ingredient.

A healthy attractional church cultivates gratitude and joy; a missional community is driven by gratitude and joy. By letting go of scarcity and fear of the unknown, the missional community walks bravely out the doors of the congregation into a world that is new and filled with possibility. Undaunted by maintenance and unfettered by structure, the missional community has a healthy dependence upon God to find a place to meet, to discover gifts from fellow travelers along the pilgrim way, and to give thanks for the joy of receiving and serving. Sometimes in cultures, especially diaspora cultures, like the church, the straw man argument sounds something like this: "They are really different, dangerous heathens out there in the big, scary world … and how they are sinful and have lost their way. We in here are much better off because we have found the truth. Poor them."

This has an interesting buffering effect on mission. It also means that people who don't feel worthy within the community can feel alone even in a group. What the missional community has the great joy and pleasure of discovering is that we are all in this together. The divide and difference between us and them is really no different at all. There's the joy of discovering that we are all fellow pilgrims and the gratitude that we are not alone is palpable in the missional community. In the darkness we discover a great light.

The missional community lives by its guts and intuition. It is in tune with imperfection. It depends upon its senses to hear, feel, and know well its mission context. It trusts that all will be well and has a hope of its future that leads it into the world. Its senses heightened, it looks for creative and innovative ways to undertake its ministry. Dependent upon the kindness of others, the community learns that dissonant voices within the attractional church are often voices of opportunity and invitation out in the world.

The missional church has very little with which to compare itself. It is unique and tied uniquely to its context. So even if the kind of ministry—a nursing home, laundry, or public space community—resembles someone else's ministry elsewhere, the reality is that it is unique because of the culture in which it is planted. This release from comparison, numbers, and statistics releases the missional community to be ever more creative.

Remember that sacraments are vessels in which grace and the Holy Spirit move. In the missional community, the sacraments of play and Sabbath are important. They allow those involved to truly find a peace outside of a culture that sets exhaustion as a status symbol and productivity as a sign of self-worth. There is no "try harder" fever here; there is a sense of being. The missional community is. It is present within the life of the community and its time. It is present in the celebrations and play that is part of life. Ministry happens in conversations at coffee shops instead of offices, on the soccer field while watching kids play on Sunday morning, and in a dialogue group after seeing a movie together. These are sacramental signs within the missional community.

Sometimes the attractional community, at its worst, tries to fill up free time with program and ministry. The missional community finds that ministry and mission happen in the midst of and alongside Sabbath and play. Missional communities that meet during the week even free up weekends in new and interesting ways.

Living up to the standards set within the attractional church can, at times, be its own anxiety-building experience. Healthy attractional churches work hard to lessen the anxiety of belonging. Freed from the large numbers and the ideas that come with going to church and knowing what to wear and what will I or they say, the missional community is welcoming by cultivating a calm and stillness of space and time. The missional community has to work hard to not replicate its sending church's DNA and fill itself with anxiety about what will or not be. The spiritual practice of the missional community is prayer, quiet, listening, and less frenetic energy. It works at being and at being in relationship, more than in doing church. It is active, but at its core, it is about finding peace in the midst of the world and discovering sanctuary in the middle of the urban or suburban jungles.

The missional community goes out and finds its shrines and temples in the world long ago abandoned by the Christians, and it pauses there and claims them saying, "This is holy space." Let us rest here for a while. Like Abram who, when he ventured from his home in the land of Uhr of the Chaldeans, went about in the wilderness but made altars to God there and marked his journey into the wild.

The missional community finds that the meaningful work it is engaged in is not ministry to or for people. Instead the missional community discovers that the meaningful work is the relationship of being in community with others. *Self-doubt, supposed to,* and *shoulds* are all left behind as the missional community ventures out into the world. Early on, when I was first learning about missional communities and listening to people who do this work, Caesar Kalinowski kept saying something that struck me as a lost phrase in the church. He kept saying, we *get* to do this. We *get* to do this. The missional community understands at the heart of its work and ministry is the reality, with joy and gratitude, it gets to be freed from church as normal and gets to do and be about relationships more than anything else.

Out of this understanding of the privilege to be in a relationship naturally flow laughter, song, and dance. My daughters have reminded me of the importance of dance, laughter, and song. We sing and dance together a lot! In the missional community, such a spirit is never controlled or prescribed to events. The healthy attractional church must always be making room within itself to dance, sing, and laugh. The missional community has these as prescriptions for normal life. These are hallmarks of the work being done well. The celebration is not one that is of the missional community, and here is the key difference. A colonizing missiology would import its celebrations, dance, and songs onto the community. The celebrations, dances, songs, and laughter flow out of the context in which the community finds itself. The dances are the community's dances, not the missionary's. The celebrations that mark the time are the community's. The songs are the community's. The laughter comes from the joy of discovering these and the joy of sharing the real world moments together.[105]

Community Principles

Brené Brown is responsible for these guideposts I have adopted for healthy attractional churches and missional communities. The point here has been to go deeper in the differences among attractional congregations and sending congregations and how missional communities are shaped within their own guideposts for health. What I deeply imagine is that Episcopal missional communities will be (like their attractional counterparts) places of wholehearted mission. I now want to offer three principles and a manifesto for our new missiology.

Brené Brown says that daring greatly is living life as enough and out of a sense of worthiness.[106] Living out that worthiness is cultivating the courage, compassion, and connection to wake up in the morning and think, No matter what gets done and how much is left undone, I am enough. It's going to bed at night thinking, Yes, I am imperfect and vulnerable and sometimes afraid, but that doesn't change the truth that I am also brave and worthy of love and belonging.[107]

I believe that God throughout the scripture and Jesus specifically repeatedly cultivated communities that are courageous in the face of the unknown, danger, fear, and future. Jesus taught specifically that his followers were to have compassion for their neighbor, just as he had compassion for those around him. Jesus removed the binding force of the law through grace and the cross. He taught us that the Sabbath was made for man and not man for the Sabbath, reminding us that ultimately we are made for God's pleasure. He told us that our sins are forgiven and, though we are forever imperfect, we are God's, part of God's family, and forever enough. The followers of Jesus are brave even though they may be afraid. The followers of Jesus understand they have been both created and redeemed, so they are worthy by their nature. The follower of Jesus understands they are worthy of love and belonging.

Rooted deep within her Episcopal Church and life experiences, along with her scientific method, Brené Brown reminds us of what our scriptures have told us all along. Brené Brown's research has shown the following:

- Love and belonging are irreducible needs of all men, women, and children. We're hardwired for connection. It gives purpose and meaning to our lives. The absence of love, belonging, and connection always leads to suffering.
- A strong belief in our worthiness doesn't just happen. It's cultivated when we understand the guideposts as choices and daily practices.
- The main concern of wholehearted men and women is living a life defined by courage, compassion, and connection.[108]

The missional community lives out these fundamental principles intentionally. The missional community members who are sent out into the world are faithful Christians who are willing to be seen and belong with others. They are willing to build a different kind of city together where belonging is the key. Baptism is the defining membership act within Christian community. The missional community, as the baptized, go out and belong to others beyond the membership boundary of baptism. They give themselves over to the community in which they reside and loosen the boundary of community intentionally so many more may belong.

Only in this may more come into membership. Only in this way does the church open itself up into the world. The sending church and its missional communities will lose itself in the world by giving itself over completely to it. It is ever becoming less of itself, more of the mysterious Christ in the world, so as to manifest and propagate Christ's self-giving love throughout society.

The missional community understands that intentionality is essential in its work. Worthiness and courage do not simply happen. They are shaped by practice. The missional community practices carefully the guideposts based upon Jesus's teaching and invitation to go out into the world. The missional community is intentional in the daily work of living out in the world and is intentional on reflecting with others about how that journey is going. Missional community members pray, eat, and talk with one another regularly.

The small group movement within the church is not new. Small groups have been a way to support the larger attractional churches by programing intimate life within the larger community. The difference between missional communities and the small group movements of the past is that the missional community group exists not as a smaller piece of a greater whole, but as a community out in the world, outside the attractional church. The missional community lives its life intimately within the framework of the world, not the church.

The missional community nurtures courage, compassion, and connection intentionally by being vulnerable. Certainly we see that the community by its nature, leaving the sending church behind, is courageous by opening itself up to the vulnerability of community life lived outside the safety of the church walls. This is true. However, the missional community members nurture a life lived as vulnerable by creating a space where life is lived intimately with others. Scripture itself is best lived when the stories of the narrative are no longer stories about people far away in another time and place, but they are stories that are intimately tied to my story.

It isn't that Abraham ventured into the wilderness, but I ventured into the wilderness like Abraham. It isn't that Peter, James, and John left their nets and safety of their homes to follow Jesus. It is rather that I have left the safety of my home church and the typical way of living life to follow Jesus like Peter, James, and John. It isn't that Jesus and the disciples fed the multitudes, but I feed them like the disciples before me. I take care of the widows and the orphans, I share my table with the stranger, and I visit the prisoners. I am living the life of the Bible by being part of the missionary community. I am vulnerable as they were, and in so doing I discover courage, compassion for others and myself, and connection with fellow pilgrims who are trying to make their way.

Missional Community Manifesto[109]

As a missional community, we will show love and care to the world around us, and we will model that within the community and without. Just as we believe that we are made worthy of God's love by virtue of our creation, we wish to share this message of worthiness with other people. While the mission community knows it is not perfect, it is clear that it is always showing self-care and compassion, embracing its imperfections as well as being compassionate, caring, and embracing of other's imperfections as it meets them in the world.

The missional community will practice courage as a small community, as Brené Brown says, "showing up, letting ourselves be seen, and honoring vulnerability. We will share our stories of struggle and strength. There will always be room in our home for both."[110] As a community welcoming the stranger, we will do the same for others.

The core of our understanding is that God wishes us to be reconciled with one another so we will be communities of compassion for ourselves and others. We will be about the work of creating a peaceful space in the world. We will do this by living with difference and celebrating our diversity. We will do this by helping to heal history.

As a missional community, we will set and respect boundaries. We will honor hard work, hope, and perseverance. Rest and play will be family values, as well as family practices.[111] As a community we will model accountability and respect. We know we will make mistakes, but we will work on amends. We know we shall watch and listen to one another and watch, listen, and learn about our community that we are serving. Our missional community will be places that know joy, practice gratitude, and learn how to be vulnerable.

Uncertainty and scarcity will visit, but as a community, we will support one another as we "draw from the spirit that is a part of our everyday life."[112] There will be tears, and we will face fear and grief. Together in our community, we will not take away pain, but instead we will sit with one another and teach one another how to feel it. "We will laugh and sing and dance and create. We will always have permission to be ourselves with each other. No matter what, you will always belong here."[113]

As a missional community, we will live with our whole heart, we will walk together into the unknown, and we will live, love, and dare greatly. We will never be perfect, but we will, as a missional community, allow the world to see us as we are, and we will hold sacred the gift of seeing Christ in you and so seeing you.[114]

Common Ground

I hear from a lot of individuals that they are concerned, as missional communities grow in popularity, there will be a drift in shared Anglican values. Or they don't think these look like the Episcopal Church they have inherited; therefore we shouldn't invest in them. This is all incorrect and probably rooted in some misconception that what congregations do is the historic norm of the church. It is also probably rooted in some need to justify expending their energies on an old model. At their best it may be a real concern over the very best of our tradition.

I certainly don't see any threat here. I don't see any loss of tradition happening presently in the emerging small batch communities I have studied. In fact they seem deeply connected with our Anglican spirituality, even if they are finding new contextual languages in which to bring that spirituality to life. They are life giving to our tradition. I do find that they have some core values as Episcopal/Anglican communities that seem to make them recognizable in the midst of the widespread growth of small Christian communities. These values are shared, and I would offer them here for your consideration.

These are Christian communities.[115] These are not communities interested in some great guiding spirit. On the contrary these communities are about Jesus. Leaders are clear that they are seeking to build and plant communities that are following God who is revealed in the person of Jesus Christ. And this Christ has offered reconciliation to the world through his work of salvation. They proclaim, in many different ways, with clarity, "Christ has died. Christ is risen. Christ will come again."

These small batch communities are scriptural. They are rooting their life and practices in the scripture. They believe their public and private beliefs, prayers, and liturgies are shaped by the regular engagement with scripture. They are trying to read, understand, mark, and discover the challenging biblical themes that enable people to live with difficult lives. They understand that the Bible enables a reflection on a very real God who is present in the transcendent recesses of human life that spends most of its time in a head disconnected from the body, other people, community, and God.

These communities are creedal. They may not all use the creeds regularly in their worship and gatherings. They do not see the creeds a specific confession to be signed or as a kind of church pledge of allegiance. They do, however, see the creed as the breadth of the whole Christian faith, which makes what they are doing catholic. They are building catholic communities rooted in a Trinitarian understanding of God, who is creator of all things, who is incarnate Son and deliverer of people and bringer of the Holy Spirit, and who sees the Holy Spirit as empowerer, binder, life-giver and community-maker. These small batch communities are attempting to bring the wholeness of God and faith into conversation with people.

Each of these communities understands they are rooted and formed by common prayer. They believe that prayer rooted in context and connected with historic and breadth of the church in prayer is powerful medicine. They believe and practice a prayer discipline that expresses belief and the connectedness of the individual with God and His community. Moreover these leaders and their people are willing to give one another room to go beyond the Book of Common Prayer so as to both breathe life into the prayer of their community and return life to the living prayer of the Episcopal Church.

These communities believe in connectedness. This is one of the reasons for this book. They are connected within the deep tradition of contextual and historic mission of the Christian Church from the very beginning. They are also connected within the Episcopal Church through the diocese and parishes to whom they owe their mission support. In this way they are deeply apostolic and catholic. They are universal in their ancient faith, in their connection globally with communities Anglican and Episcopal. They are connected to the oversight and pastoral relationship of bishops. In fact many small batch communities long for this very thing, and if we would but engage them, we might find a lot of communities presently disconnected who would love nothing more than to enter the fold of the Episcopal and Anglican churches.

I have already pointed out that these communities are Trinitarian. This is not some distant, foreign, or dead theology. As an aside, twenty years ago, I heard a lot of talk about getting rid of the trinity as a doctrine. What a mistake that would be! Our very life as Anglicans and Episcopalians is rooted on this deep theology because buried within it is an understanding that Christian faith is everywhere and in every expression relational. God is revealed in the Holy Trinity and is understood as relational. The hospitality of God and the economic outflowing of God causes not only creation to be birthed but also brings forth community. God's all-encompassing love and outpouring of self in order to be in community with creation and creature is an inclusive invitation to step over the boundaries that prevent community from happening. The very nature of small batch embraces a theology of inclusivity and relationship as a priority and key ingredient to life. The God of love is interested in our loving of the other—all others.

Lastly these communities also share the value that they are not only unapologetically Christian but are unapologetically evangelistic. While recognizing that they are in fact working out their own salvation, these leaders are fearless! They are humble, they are continually placing their own lives in front of the God of love, and they are truly open to God's spiritual forgiveness and guidance. At the same time, they believe, by doing this work, their own spiritual lives are being enlivened. They are all called to take their experience of a God of love out into the world. They are willing to travel beyond the confines of the church boundaries, church walls, and normal church life and share with those they find out in the world. They believe their faith comes alive as they encounter the other person on the street, in the coffee shop, in the veterans group, in the Laundromat, and in the prison.

These gifted missionaries, for there is no other word for them, are committed to traveling out of the land of comfort into the land of people who are making their way unaccompanied by Jesus. And there in the midst of the world, they go to set up altars, like Abram as he ventured from the land of Ur of the Chaldeans. These people know—they believe—the marrow of their bones flows with the simple belief that speaking and doing the message of freedom in Jesus is what it is all about. Regardless of mission engagement—justice, environment, community organizing, house groups, conversations, shared pilgrimage, and all the many different ways they are making small batch communities—these people are sharing the Good News.

They inspire me. We should be doing everything we can as an organized denominational church to support these entrepreneurial individuals who are reclaiming the work of missionary as a vocation in our church and showing us the way into the future. My pledge as bishop is to make room, give cover, inspire, empower, and support with time, energy, and money this work. Here lies a key to the living future of the church fifty years from now. Here lies the beating heart of mission. Here we can see God's hand at work in the world around us. And we should pay attention.

Dispatches from the Front: The Southside Abbey

Let me introduce to you The Reverend Robert K. Leopold, missioner in the Episcopal Diocese of East Tennessee and founder of Southside Abbey. You can make your online pilgrimage here, www.southsideabbey.org. *This is their story.*

So much of what they do at Southside Abbey comes from their community context. Essentially they are a nontraditional worshipping community in the Episcopal tradition. Half of their worshipping community are homeless or in transitional housing (car, motel, camps, and so forth) of some kind. There is diversity of most every kind. They have immigrants from El Salvador, Guatemala, Cuba, Russia, Sudan, Ethiopia, Kenya, Burundi, and even north of the Mason-Dixon line. They have PhDs and folks who struggle with literacy. There are millionaires from Lookout Mountain and those experiencing homelessness. It is the closest, Leopold remarks, that he has seen to what Bishop Tutu describes as "the Rainbow People of God."

How It Began

Southside Abbey describes itself as a worshipping community in the Episcopal tradition that is being created by the people of the Southside, a diverse urban neighborhood in Chattanooga, Tennessee. It's where they celebrate the Eucharist as a meal together every Friday night. It's where—with worship, community, presence, and volunteering—community members follow Jesus, love their neighbors, and change the world. Southside Abbey is just beginning. Leopold writes,

> It's an experiment, it's messy, it's fun—and it is full of possibility and hope. We are transformational, sustainable, and replicable. When I go talk about Southside Abbey, one of my main points (after Holy Spirit, the Jesus Movement, the Love of God, and good stuff like that) is that people can do this kind of ministry—it can be done."

They are a model of how to be an Episcopal church without a building, made up of many who pronounce the word *'piscopal*. Their innovations are essentially innovations of structure, not content. As such, they share all they develop. You can go to their website and find their founding documents, liturgies, music, and their budget and use it freely. Just look under the open source tab.

What They Learned

1. They would barter for free space. Some Episcopalian or Lutheran somewhere must have space on the Southside someplace.
2. They would have a team of clergy involved, not just one person. Specifically a vocational deacon would have done much to foster the team approach to leadership early in our history.
3. They would have offered the food family-style from the beginning. They started with a line, which, even though people served themselves, felt very soup-kitcheny.
4. Leopold says he doesn't really know what this looks like, but they could have done more with making those with homes feel safe and welcome when our community grew to include those experiencing homelessness.

What They Might Do Differently

In reflecting about their ministry, Leopold believes they could do a better job of promoting themselves. They must come to an understanding that promotion of their community is part of the promotion of Jesus.

At the same time, they should have realized that what they offer is not for everyone. There are some who would never be comfortable within the framework of their Friday evening service but are intrigued by what they do. If they could organize sharing their message and their mission, they could raise a bit more money and expand their community.

Their biggest challenge moving forward is this development work. Sustainability has been the toughest for them. As it turns out, a worshipping community such as Southside Abbey is not self-sustaining. They can't have what many Episcopalians think of as church without a lot of money. While they have managed to eliminate much of the costs associated with an Episcopal Church, they still have the monumental cost that is the clergy.

They have grown too big for their small space. They have grown too big for their small budget. They have grown too broad in scope for their small town. They have to find some way to make those sought-after demographics of twentysomethings and young families more comfortable in worship, and they need to do a better job of explaining their dreams to people who could help fund their mission.

Questions

1. What does the word *missiology* mean to you? What do you see as the primary difference between an attractional missiology and the missiology of a small batch community? What are the similarities?
2. Bishop Doyle says "the attractional community's future is certain, healthy, and viable." Do you agree? If so, why are missional communities still important?
3. Where do you more expect to encounter Jesus Christ: inside the walls of the church or out in the world? Why?
4. Bishop Doyle says the church must embrace her imperfections. Do you agree? How might embracing our imperfections enhance the church's mission?

Recommendations for Further Reading

Book of the Acts of the Apostles

- Those guys and ladies just went for it. They trusted that God would provide, and God did.

Generous Orthodoxy by Brian McLaren

Falling Upward by Richard Rohr

Leaving Church by Barbara Brown Taylor

Chapter 8

Small Batch Leadership

In the fourth century, the Church of Milan did a crazy thing. It elected an unbaptized Christian as their bishop because that particular individual was exactly who the church needed in order to fulfill God's mission. The Church of Milan was made up of cities of many different sizes that included Liguria and Emilia. Milan had several monuments and was a populous city. There were imperial palaces and a complex of wealthy Roman homes with a thriving population.[116] It was a region of great commerce and the center of Roman authority. The urban Christians of the time met in all kinds of places from synagogues and homes to public spaces. It was a time of great growth and expansion. There was a growth in the formalization of Christianity as we have discussed. It was also a time of numerous clergy and large communities. The diocese was, by this time, a large geographical area. This thriving diocese, with growth, commerce, and political power, did this crazy thing. They elected a man called Ambrose to be their bishop. Today we call him St. Ambrose.

St. Ambrose was a Roman citizen. He grew up sometime around 340 AD. His father was a prefect of Gaul, and his mother was a devoted Christian. Ambrose, like his father before him, was educated and studied literature, law, and rhetoric.[117] He made his way into politics and eventually became a prefect or governor himself. He was to oversee Liguria and Emilia on behalf of the Roman state from his headquarters in Milan.

We might imagine, from an early stage in life, his mother too had an influence on him. We know he was participating in the catechumenate, the preparation for baptism, while in Milan.[118] The catechumenate at this time was a lengthy process lasting three years. He found himself in the middle of the Arian controversy, the controversy of the day.[119] As governor, he had to deal with the disruption as it played out in the civic world too, for church and politics are siblings that have never gotten along particularly well. In the middle of this furor, the bishop of Milan, an Arian, died. We can imagine that Ambrose as a neophyte, and as governor, he went to a meeting where they were to elect the bishop's replacement out of pure religious and political curiosity. He may have even hoped, as governor, he might be able to keep the different parties from devolving into violence. People on both sides of the controversy turned to Ambrose and decided to elect him as their bishop.[120] Evidently everyone thought this might bring peace including, the emperor, Valentinian II. The problem was, of course, that Ambrose was not a baptized Christian.

Ambrose pleaded that the orthodox canon did not allow neophytes to be ordained. He was put under house arrest and eventually conceded. The bishops agreed to put aside the canons and to make room for Ambrose's ordination.[121] He was baptized. The Christian historian Paulinus, in *Life of Ambrose*, records what happened next. Evidently the bishops were willing to set aside the requirements for ordination but not the preparation. Therefore, Ambrose, following his baptism, spent each day fulfilling all of the varying ecclesiastical offices. This means that Ambrose spent time serving in every church grade from doorkeeper to priest.[122] It turns out that Ambrose was just what the church needed at that time. He had the gifts and was able to lead the church through a difficult and trying time.

The goal of the future church will be to find and work with individuals of every kind who already work well and are committed to the positive future of the church. Regardless of education, credentials, jobs, and pay, the future church sees everyone as a missionary of God's reconciling work. It is not a church where clericalism is disguised as the ministry of the baptized.

In the ancient models, leadership was neighborhood-oriented. This meant that you found the leaders in the people who were connected to your family or your business or were invested in your community. The future church finds its leaders from every part of society, regardless of background and time within the community. The future church builds collaborative leadership across geographical boundaries and is not limited to one-on-one relationships but amplifies them through electronic means. In our "back to the future" models, we will have more Ambrose-type leaders. The ancient church and its leadership were wise enough to figure out how they were going to enable the person with the gifts needed by the church to serve. This will be the way of the future Episcopal Church.

People who serve in the church will be of every age. While there is a resurgence in ordinations of young people, there will continue to be older clergy ordinations. Longer and healthier life spans and the trend toward second careers and multiple avocations will continue to have a strong affect. The bishops, priests, and deacons of the future church will be full time, part time, and nonstipendiary. The greater numbers will be part time and nonstipendiary. There will be deacons and priests who are doctors, lawyers, mechanics, waiters, and hairdressers. There will also be vocations that are full time and serve in greater capacities to undertake the wider church organization. In the future church, the full-time ministers will be far outnumbered by the part-time ones. This will be true not because of a small and shrinking church.

The seminary of the future will focus on training both lay and ordained for mission. Providing a new learning ecology online with inexpensive tools and new ways of creating learning space and collaboration will all be the hallmarks of the future seminary. The seminary will understand that there is a new wave of makers who are invested in seeing the future church alive and flourishing. The makers are willing to do what they need to do, and the future seminary is ready to help empower them, raising the best spiritually and theologically prepared missionaries. Regardless of whether or not the student is to be bivocational or full time, the seminary of the future will help to ensure that the future missionary is undergirded with sound biblical scholarship, healthy ministry practices, and a wealth of resources to form unabashed Episcopalians.

There are some artifacts of the future seminary in our midst. Over ten years ago, Mary MacGregor and I, along with a few others, gathered in a room and came up with a theological school concept for training laity and clergy. MacGregor did the lion's share of the work and brought life to the IONA School. The Diocese of Texas created a way to train bivocational clergy who could not leave their homes and their employment for three years to attend residential seminary. The Reverend Sam Todd joined the effort and put together a brilliant faculty to teach. The team is largely made up of PhDs who are adjunct or retired seminary/university faculty members. Today, thanks to the innovation of The Right Reverend Dena Harrison and in collaboration with the Seminary of the Southwest in Austin, the school has spread to over ten dioceses. This year the IONA school and its partnership, the IONA Initiative, trained over 110 people for ministry. This number does not include the lay and clergy tracks running at the seminary. Together we are training over two hundred people for ministry in a variety of forms. This is a great example of how seminaries can redefine themselves and serve as a learning hub for the wider church.

The future of the school will be dependent on how well it begins to multiply itself online and create real-time community among the different schools for mutual and shared learning. Other dioceses are starting local schools also. These are smaller, regional collaborations that are more pliable than the former seminary type structures. Trinity School for Ministry was an early adopter of online training in our denomination; others are following. This is a place where seminaries could learn from one another and share their experiences in order to improve accessibility across all of the seminaries. Numerous lay programs are popping up across seminary campuses. These tend to be regional and largely inaccessible to people who do not live in the local area. How well the seminaries open up these programs online will gauge their long-term participation in the future seminary movement. There are also seminaries experimenting with new models of library accessibility, like the eBook reader project in the province of South Africa. There is a shortage of librarians to take care of the massive number of theological texts filling libraries that remain largely inaccessible to students in the vast areas of Africa. The Right Reverend Dr. Thabo Makgoba has launched a project that will give access to students of the great theological and other libraries of the world.[123] In 2014 Virginia Theological Seminary held an eformation conference that shared media-rich formation tools. They held the gathering as a learning lab. Acting as a resource, the seminary offered a vision of how cultural shifts are changing the way individuals engage the spiritual journey. Imagine how eformation might shape leaders across a missionary diocese and provide curricula and training along with small group tools for building a community of interconnected lay and ordained small batch leaders.

L. Gregory Jones is vice president and vice provost for global strategy and programs at Duke University, where he is also professor of theology in the Divinity School. In the magazine *The Christian Century*, he writes to the present-day seminaries and their leadership, "Incremental changes are insufficient."[124] The changing missionary context is causing "tectonic" shifts.[125] He lists

> the digital revolution; the emergence of a "multimodal" world of complicated ethnic relationships and cultural dynamics, both within the United States and globally; changing patterns of denominations and new forms of congregating; the questioning of—and cynicism about—institutions; economic stresses on Christian organizations that challenge old business models and press issues of sustainability; shifting vocations of laypeople; and the lure of cities.[126]

Jones calls for "clarity about why theological education is important and a willingness to experiment—and to experiment in ways richly connected to the best of our traditions."[127]

The future church will require its seminaries and schools to be part of the education of the larger population of do-it-yourself (DIY) missionaries. Creating small batch communities will require us to reshape how we raise up and train people. These will be amplified Christians who are eager to innovate, design, modify, and make things on their own and in collaborative groups for the sake of God's mission of reconciliation.[128] The future church, the future seminary, must value open collaboration. It will tap into networks and platforms that enable self-organizing structures for local adaption. It will be this way because the church has removed its hold on vocations and is growing through many and varied small batch ministries.

The church will always have professional full-time clergy and pay them, but a new variety is here to stay, and it will not regress. Without this diverse model of vocations, the mission of the church is jeopardized. An approach to small batch ministries, congregational vitality, and new sending church models will mean that Christian communities will be of many and varied types. Think about what this approach will mean for the shape of leadership.

The amplified missional church will raise up clergy who will work in a variety of contextual settings. In a suburban community, the future church may be organized with a full-time priest serving with several nonstipendiary priests who help with the wider sacramental and pastoral responsibilities of the growing community and its multiple sites. Meanwhile in the same parish community, a nonstipendiary priest and several deacons might be out starting new communities in underserved areas and creating service connections throughout the surrounding neighborhood. In an urban context, we might find a nonstipendiary priest and deacon working in a slum, or poorer part of town, to build up a Christian community around an organized project, like a community garden to provide fresh fruit and vegetables in the middle of a food desert. They might be sponsored and connected with a larger community like the one mentioned above, or they might be stand-alone. A large urban parish may have several full-time priests and deacons, an army of nonstipendiary clergy, and a host of lay preachers, pastors, and administrators who oversee multiple mission sites and a variety of small congregation/communities across the whole city. Still a small community congregation may have a full-time priest or be served by an urban or suburban nonstipendiary leader.

All of these scenarios of the future church will share resources and build ministry capacity by sharing administration and overhead. There will be bishops who have several dioceses that they help to oversee. Nonstipendiary and part-time bishops will join them to help increase the pastoral reach. Gone are the days of concern over numbers of bishops representing dioceses.

Missionary bishops working in teams and sharing the work of the episcopate will replace the "full-time one bishop to a diocese" model.

Bishops will raise up and call forth a diverse clergy and lay population focused on the mission of the new church. There will be bishops who hold positions as heads of congregations and large urban communities. There will be bishops who travel and make as their vocation the support of new ministry contexts where various creative and innovative styles of leadership are needed to propel ministry forward. There is no one solution or idea with which the future church carries out its ministry. It does all things necessary for the sake of the God's mission of reconciliation.

When it comes to leadership, the driving force will be the amplification of mission. No longer will the church raise up leaders for the maintenance of communities but instead for the vitality of existing congregations, the multiplication of communities, and the diversification of DIY small batch mission.

Dispatches from the Front: Broadmoor Community Start-up

Let me introduce to you Bob Lowry, a deacon at Holy Comforter in Spring, Texas, just outside of Houston. His community does not have a website because his community is at the Broadmoor Nursing Home at Creekside in Spring. *This is their story.*

Lowry and his rector, Jimmy Abbot, were thinking about planting a community in an assisted living facility. What they knew after visiting was that most all of them had services of some kind in most facilities and were provided by churches in the area. Still others had television evangelists piped into the unit by television. Some churches provided volunteers that would do Bible study or Sunday afternoon service.

How It Began

They found the Broadmoor at Creekside in Spring under construction. Bob called on the new managing director and asked if he could hold a Sunday morning service, and she agreed. They are now in their second year with some interesting results. They have regularly twenty-five to thirty-five in attendance. The majority of those who attend are residents, but families and caretakers also attend.

What They Learned

Bob says, "These folks would go unchurched if we did not provide one for them." Also it is not an outreach to their Holy Comforter folks at Creekside. This is a very real mini church plant within an assisted living community.

What They Might Do Differently

The mission could be enlarged. Lowry would like to see a brochure created that could be used at other facilities to attest to their success as they look for additional opportunities. Also he would put more emphasis on Sunday morning services and include allowing his laity to participate, preach, and lead the service. None of the other churches are paying attention to live services or the natural time for most people to attend church. He believes their laity would get much more out of attending church if they were leading and preaching. Then Bob could relieve them from time to time, or someone could agree to float among facilities that could help with the Eucharist.

Today there are four other communities experimenting with this kind of intentional community. They are using many different ways of gathering. However, each has in common a desire to not only hold worship but to build up weekly pastoral care and ministry by the participants themselves, as well as Bible study groups. We will know these communities truly become missional when they do their work without a team coming in and doing it for them. Instead there will be a community there in which their missionaries feel as though they are participating in creating with those they are serving.

Questions

1. Bishop Doyle notes how the Church of Milan broke with tradition to elect Ambrose as bishop. What traditions might today's church consider breaking for the sake of mission amplification?
2. What does the word *leadership* mean to you? How is the nature of leadership changing? What skills or character traits will leaders in the future church need to possess in order to be effective?
3. Bishop Doyle says "there is no one solution or idea with which the future church carries out its ministry." Do you agree? If so, does this statement excite you or make you anxious? Why?
4. What potential gifts might a greater number of part-time and nonstipendiary clergy bring to the future church? How will this shift impact lay leadership in the church?

Recommendations for Further Reading

Get a Grip on Your Business by Gino Wickman

Launching Missional Communities by Mike Breen

The Pilgrim Church by E. H. Broadbent

Chapter 9

Starting Your Small Batch Community

After several years of casting a vision for small batch communities and deepening our understanding of the new forms of Christian community we're taking on, I invited the clergy of the Diocese of Texas to help me plant small Christian communities. Today our diocese has five congregations who have started small batch communities that have grown into their own small congregations as second site ministries. We have also started planting congregations and are hoping over the next decade to plant twenty-five new congregations. As we do this work, we have set a goal to plant fifty small batch communities in five years, and we are well on our way.

Today we have fifteen in various forms of start-up. As you think about joining what is a movement across the Episcopal Church and has been a Christian tradition since our very first days of following Jesus, you will want to think about steps or stages in the process. What follows is an idea about how you might begin. Everyone does it differently, so think about this as an unimproved trail of sorts into the world of small batch Christian communities.

Step One: Be Clear

Be clear about what you are doing. Be honest about expectations. Build a team that understands what their work is clearly to be about. Remember that a missional community in our tradition is a group of Episcopalians about the size of an extended family, who are sent out and off campus by a sending church (or, in some traditions, called the "anchor church"), united and empowered by common prayer/worship and Bible study and in service to a particular neighborhood or network of relationships.

It is never fully a missional community until people from the community (nonchurch members) join the life and work of the new start. These communities are focused on caring for/blessing/serving a particular group together and celebrating/breaking bread with the particular group. Missional communities are made up of individuals who are equipped through the story of the Anglican faith and sent out to make community in the world and to serve those whom they encounter. This is not a Bible study or a small group. As Kalinowski writes, "Rather, it applies to the whole life of every believer. Every disciple is to be an agent of the kingdom of God, and every disciple is to carry the mission of God into every sphere of life."[129]

Remember that laypeople can start a missional community. Over the past few chapters, some of you have indeed received a vision and a gift of the Holy Spirit that has called you to do this work. Many others of you also had clarity that your work is to be the protective anchor church member who is to help launch a missional community but will live your life within the attractional church. Both of these callings are valid. Therefore pause and take a deep breath, and let us think a bit about some process points to help further discernment. It is always a good thing to remember that moving slowly, deliberately, and with prayer and discernment is the best way.[130]

Step Two: Pray for Discernment

Regardless of where you find yourself in this process, join me in praying for discernment about this work of multiplying our gospel witness throughout the world. We don't need to know what to do right now. We don't even need to answer who and where. Simply begin by praying and wondering with God where God will invite us to start a small batch missional community.

Step Three: Thoughtfully Consider and Pray That Those Who Are to Be Sent Will Be Made Known to You

Who in your current community might be good evangelists and partners? Who is being called? Remember, that may be you too.

Step Four: Get Local

Pray about what kind of community you are called to create. Are you or your sending church community being called to

- create communities that are like house churches serving a neighborhood;
- create communities of service or monastic community of individuals living together;
- start an Episcopal Young Adult Service Corps community like the Bayou City Service Corps, or something similar;
- create a community within a nursing home;
- create a community within an apartment complex;
- create a community within a prison;
- create a campus community at a local college;
- plant a community based upon music and art;
- engage and create a community around reflection and discussion;
- create a community within or alongside a service organization or nongovernmental organization (NGO);
- create a second campus ministry
- partner/restart a rural community or adopt a smaller congregation; or
- create a service community as a second site congregation

Step Five: Get Organic

While discerning the kind of community you want to start, who is being sent, and who is going, begin to pray that you will have clarity about where and for understanding about the service opportunities and how your missional community might bless, give, and serve their neighbor. Don't ask what you can do for the community, but seek instead to discover who the community is and where you might see a community sprouting up. Go deep and remember to be pliable.

Step Six: Formation

Pray and discern how you might gather. What forms of prayer root your community? What are your community's practices that undergird the work you are to do?

Step Seven: Get Sustainable

Invite your anchor congregation to begin to pray for this mission and the people involved. Remember that you are being sent and you do not need a huge infrastructure. Start small and sustainable. Bigger projects, like coffee shops and second sites, may take start-up money. Figure out your strategy and your funding model.

Step Eight: Help Manage/Guide Your Mission Community

Help manage/guide your mission community team in the development of a plan and launch.

Step Nine: Have Your Sending Church Hold a Service

Have your sending church hold a service where the community commissions these apostles to go out. Help the congregation understand what they are doing and where they are going.

Step Ten: Report Back

Report back regularly to your congregation. Dispatches from the front inspire and ignite other mission efforts. Let the sending church know what the small batch is doing and how they are doing. Let them know what is happening and how they can help you.

There are many books on steps that you might want to consult. They are listed below. You might also talk with some of the people mentioned in this book to gain ideas about your potential work. What is important is for you to take this nine-point plan and use it as a skeleton to develop your own strategic missional community plant. You must have a business model of some kind that clearly defines the work.

What is essential is that you know and understand that you are creating a missional community and not a greenfield. A greenfield is always an attractional church tool, and it will require a completely different set of guidelines and goals. Remember that you are sending out missionaries to create in the world a new small batch community that is local, organic, and sustainable.

Dispatches from the Front: Bushwick Abbey

Let me introduce to you The Reverend Kerlin Richter, the founder of Bushwick Abbey in Bushwick-Brooklyn-New York. You can make your online pilgrimage here, http://bushwickabbey.org. *This is their story.*

Bushwick Abbey is unapologetically Christian, which means they believe they stand on holy ground and meet people where they are. They are a welcoming community to all. They are persuaded that neither death, life, angels, principalities, powers, things present or to come, height, depth, nor any other creature shall be able to separate us from the love of God, which is in Christ Jesus our Lord. So they seek to model this radical inclusiveness.

How It Began

Richter started her work with Bushwick Abbey in June 2013 while she was still a transitional deacon. She did monthly vespers and community events until December of that year when they started weekly services and she was ordained to the priesthood. For the first year, they met in a bar, which closed due to legal trouble. And since November 2014, they have met in the parish hall of their Spanish-speaking sister church. They are currently somewhere between twenty-five to forty average Sunday attendance, mostly folks in their twenties to early thirties. An online article written by Nekoro Gomes in 2014 characterizes Bushwick this way,

> When most people think of Bushwick these days, the words *Christian fellowship* do not exactly jump into the imagination. For many younger Christian transplants to the city it can be hard to find a welcoming place of worship, especially one that forgives the trespasses of young Brooklynites—rolling out of bed after 10, quite possibly showing up hungover, and not donning their "Sunday best." That's where Bushwick Abbey, a new Episcopal church based on values of community, acceptance, and modern living, stands out. The self-proclaimed "Church That Doesn't Suck" service takes place every Sunday in the unlikely holy space of music venue Radio Bushwick. When Pastor Kerlin Richter realized that there were no English-speaking Episcopal congregations in Bushwick closer than the Halsey L stop, she created a new church where parishioners of all faiths, ethnicities, and sexual orientations are "welcome to participate and bring [their] whole selves."[131]

Kerlin Richter has a great spirit, and her answers to our questions were wonderful.

What They Learned

1. You must love the people you are working with.
2. Some things will be easier if the founder is from the same or similar culture as the people you are called to. There is something profoundly invitational about unchurched folks encountering someone like them who is already a lover of Jesus (female, queer, tattooed, young, alter-abled, of color, or whatever).
3. Let go of Episcopal identity as primary identity. Focus on Christian faith. It's very important for me to be solid in my tradition, but people do not join Bushwick Abbey to become Episcopalians.

That said, I think my people love that we have the larger church behind us.
4. Church planting is hard.
5. Partners would have been great. You will need highly social extroverted people to do this work, and we struggle with working alone. I love to process ideas out loud and in conversation.
6. Use the press. Get yourself out there. Every mention is a chance for someone who needs you to find you.
7. Get out. Go to coffee shops, bars, shows, or wherever life actually revolves around in your neighborhood.
8. My people place a high value in inclusivity and partying in art, music, and justice. So we try to focus on that stuff a lot. If I were in a place with a bunch of kids or people who knit, our community life would look different.
9. There is a tension between organic growth and strategic planning. Be intentional without stifling the spirit with numbers. My ELCA friends have a struggle with this.
10. Neighborhood, neighborhood, neighborhood. You may not have an office. Go to coffee shops, bars, parks, and libraries.
11. Wear your collar. Yes, it's uncomfortable. Just wear it and be your freaky Jesus-loving self on full display in unexpected places. The people need to know there is a priest in their midst.
12. The whole church needs to be visible. Live sacramental life. Show outward and visible signs. We can't do that locked inside.
13. Be like Reverend MacGyver. I bet you have more tools for ministry lying around than you think at first. Who do you know, and what do you have that can be used for creative ministry?
14. Join up with what is already happening. You don't have the energy to reinvent the wheel. Who is already doing good work in your neighborhood: after-school programs, eco-justice, or whatever? Show up and help out. Be humble and willing to learn.
15. Be curious. Fall in love with the actual people in front of you, not who you think should be there or who the demographic studies told you would be there, but the real-life, living, breathing, broken, and beautiful people God has sent you.
16. Pray for your people, your church, and yourself.
17. Pray more.
18. Take risks, trust people, and be okay with failure. If the gospel is preached even once to someone who needs to hear it, how can we fail?

19. Don't worry if people have no experience. Jump in the deep end, and trust them.
20. What is already happening in the neighborhood? Is there an arts festival? You should have a booth.
21. Do your research. Reach out, and listen to the stories of both the newcomers and the old-timers. Don't jump to conclusions about what your neighborhood needs. Short of proclaiming the Good News, be cautious, especially if you are white. White people have a terrible habit of trying to fix things they don't fully understand.
22. In a chaotic world, disruptions and curiosity can be a tool. Use whatever you've got. Be weird. It opens up space.
23. Say yes to invitations and ideas. This is part of being willing to fail.
24. Talk about money, stewardship, and gratitude early and often. Don't be embarrassed to share your theology of stewardship. The church being ashamed of its generosity and its need serves no one.
25. It has been wonderful to partner with an existing church but also have lots of freedom. I think this can go either way, but the priest and community at the (sending) "big sister" church needs to be secure enough not to get threated by new growth not under its control.
26. I have fantastic friends and mentors who have done this work before, and I most certainly stay curious about what others are doing, including Nadia Bolz-Webber in Denver, Emily Scott here in New York, and Karen Ward's work in Seattle. I also have a good friend in Portland who started an Evangelical Covenant Church that failed after five years.
27. It's great to look to other communities, but make sure your curiosity is as much about the questions they are asked as the answers they came up with. For example, Nadia at HFASS does the blessing of the bicycles. Instead of saying, "Oooh, cool idea. Let's copy it and do our own blessing of the bicycles," instead ask, "What are the main cultural identifiers of my neighborhood and my people? How do they identify themselves, and what of those pieces might they think have nothing to do with church? How can we bless those places in their lives so we can profess with more than words that, as incarnational people, our whole lives are holy and worthy of blessing? What has maybe never been blessed in your neighborhood?
28. It's not necessarily a contradictory idea, but copy stuff that other churches are doing. If it sounds good, try it.

29. Let your liturgy grow out of your context. The brilliance of the Episcopal Church is that it is like the hydrangea. It can change color depending on the soil it's planted in. We do not lose our identity by worshipping in the vernacular; rather our identity is all about being contextual.
30. There is a huge gift in trusting gentle oversight. Pick people you trust and then trust them. It is empowering and liberating not to be anxious when your boss comes around. I have been truly blessed by having Stephanie Spellers and Bishop Provenzano. They have trusted me to do this work, and I have never doubted that they have my back.[132]

Questions

1. What excites you about the potential of starting a new small batch community? What scares you?
2. If you were to start a new missional community, who in your community might make good partners?
3. What support from your congregation do you need to start a new missional community?
4. Who in your community is most in need of being blessed and served by the church? Think of three practical ways that a new missional community might serve and bless this particular group of people.

Recommendations for Further Reading

"The Toynbee Convector," a short story by Ray Bradbury

The Celtic Way of Evangelism by George Hunter

Chapter 10

Three From The Beginning

A New Beginning in Del Valle, Austin, Texas

"In 1991 the bus from my East Austin junior high would take hours to reach my West Austin home. The route began with a few drop offs in streets immediately surrounding Kealing Middle School, but soon dipped South, and wound circuitously through the seemingly endless barrios of East Austin before curving back to my neck of the woods. On this drive, we'd pass an endless array of piñata stores, carnicerías and panaderías. Parents waiting for their children would greet them exclusively in Spanish, and Norteño and Banda thundered out of every passing truck," wrote The Reverend Bertie Pearson, reflecting on the change in the area.

Today, nearly twenty-five years later, the carnicería has been replaced by an artisanal butcher, the piñata shop is flanked by vintage boutiques, and kids of every ethnicity file out of buses at those same stops. Over the last two decades, the historic Latino areas of South and East Austin have shifted from sitting beyond the red line of middle-class desirability to being among the chicest zip codes in Austin, and thousands of working poor families have fallen victim to skyrocketing rents and property taxes. The barrios are barrios no more.

Austin's recent prosperity has meant a shortage of affordable housing, and for many Latino families pushed out of South and East Austin, relocating within the city is no longer an option. Many members of San Francisco de Asís that began as neighbors of the original South 1st Street church building have moved out to the semi-rural township of Del Valle, nearly an hour's drive from the church. Many of these families continue to make the trek to San Francisco each Sunday, but others have found the commute too much of an obstacle, and their attendance has become sparser with each passing year.

In early 2015, Petra Perez, a San Francisco de Asís leader who was part of this migration, said, "Padre, what would you think about holding a service on my back porch?"

She said that many families still considered San Francisco their home, but due to lack of transportation, the price of gas, and so forth, they just couldn't make it to church. Petra also did a little research in her neighborhood and found this to be a common problem among her neighbors. Many were new transplants who had left behind churches in Austin to find that Del Valle offered only a small Roman Catholic mission visited by a priest on Saturdays and a Charismatic Evangelical storefront church. She felt that beginning a mission in Del Valle would be a great service, not only to our former members but to all of her neighbors.

Petra's husband Angel enclosed their large back porch to protect them from rain and heat, and they began holding a service of Holy Communion at 7:00 p.m. on the last Sunday of the month, followed by a shared meal. They invited both the Del Valle and Austin members of the church and got a commitment from several San Francisco de Asís families to attend monthly and help build a critical mass. They've been at it for six months, and it's been a wonderful experience. Some months they get a lot of locals and other months. It's Petra's family and a few members of San Francisco, but gathering for worship in their little porch-chapel, looking out over the fields of Del Valle, never fails to be a wonderful experience.

Pearson says his missiology is well summed up in Washington Phillip's classic 1929 jam *Lift Him Up* (https://www.youtube.com/watch?v=SBpfdjpBniM).

> Oh, lift Him up that's all
> Lift Him up in His Word
> If you'll tell the Name of Jesus everywhere
> If you'll keep His Name a-ringin' everywhere that you go
> He will draw men unto Him.

Mosaic: A Missional Community in Pearland, Texas

Debbie Allensworth, with the guidance and support of The Reverend Jim Liberatore, has planted a small batch community in Pearland, Texas. Mosaic is a community outreach–centered second campus of St. Andrew's in Pearland. The west side of Pearland is a very diverse community with not much interest in organized church, but with a passion for finding ways to make a difference to other people. Their church community at the Mosaic campus is small but willing to pitch in to serve others in new and creative ways. Worship is interactive and often involves videos and always involves discussions and feedback.

The seed of Mosaic got started around 2005 when St. Andrew's began a series of shutting down Sunday worship at the church building and moving into the community on Sunday morning. They began the journey of seeing the church as a people and not as a building. They began to be more people-centered rather than building-centered. This outward emphasis took three forms:

1. They moved worship into homes and parks over an entire weekend. There were eleven services over three days and four nights. People saw the dominical day (a Sabbath day) as flexible in the age of weekend sports and getaways for over scheduled families. This worship outside the walls took place one to two times a year. People were encouraged to invite their neighbors.
2. They moved off Sunday campus worship to service projects all over the weekend. Each project drew parishioners and their friends to an area of ability and interest. All ages and abilities had a choice of projects. Worship was moved to a short service at the projects' sites rather than at the church building.
3. They encouraged people who needed the weekend off to take worship with them where they went. Youth worshipped at the beach. Parents worshipped with their families at the campgrounds. They trained team members to be lay Eucharistic visitors so communion could be a part of their experience.

As a result of these three streams of parish life, they began to look at serving West Pearland. They knew, since the mid-1990s, this area was going to grow rapidly and be underserved spiritually. They also knew the area west of Highway 288 would be different: different ethnic makeup, different school district, as well as different work and shopping patterns. From West Pearland, it took over twenty-five minutes to get to the 518 campus. They saw Mosaic as a solution to serving a spiritually isolated group that would most likely not travel to East Pearland to worship, if they thought about worship at all. They approached the Diocese of Texas about having a second campus in West Pearland. This campus would not have to duplicate the entire infrastructure of a new church and could make use of existing staff and volunteers for development. They subsequently rented retail space (3,200 square feet) on a main highway in West Pearland.

They received two grants and, with the backing of the existing congregation, chose to reach out to the west side of the city. This is the fastest-growing area in Pearland, and those on the west side rarely travel east into old Pearland, instead heading north into Houston or staying local to the west side to shop, eat, and so forth so many rarely drove by our 518 campus. They chose to focus on outreach or service to others in order to help people from the community find ways to engage in serving others alongside the members of the congregation. They have learned a lot about renting commercial property and outfitting a campus and are still learning about advertising in a budget-friendly but still effective way.

Mosaic is a service community that worships rather than our 518 campus, which is a worshipping community that serves. The Mosaic campus was started with the focus not on themselves but on their neighbors. Building faithful relationships/friendships is critical. Mosaic is about loving God though neighbor love.

The Front Porch

The Front Porch seeks to engage the many different voices in their notably weird, artistically inclined, postmodernized city. Each month they host multiple gatherings at different venues across Austin to get folks talking and connecting.

While the Front Porch didn't incorporate as an official nonprofit until 2009, it began around 2000 as an informal gathering of friends who met weekly at various coffee shops, bars, and galleries to talk about stuff. This came to be affectionately called "the front porch" and included fellow Episcopal priests, UT students and professors, journalists, engineers, entrepreneurs, writers, artists, and the like. The Reverend Steve Kinney was working on his PhD at UT during this phase, studying postmodern culture, human development, dialogue, and communion in marriages, so the weekly gatherings became a sort of living laboratory for those gathered to think about Gen-X culture and the emerging church, new ways of thinking about truth as relational, and building community through dialogical interaction. It was fun and energizing, especially because people like The Reverends Jimmy Bartz, Todd Fitzgerald, Pittman McGehee, Miles Brandon, Patrick Hall, John Newton, and other lay folks were part of it in those early years.

One of many formative turning points occurred at a Bill Frisell concert at the Continental Club on South Congress Avenue. Bartz, Fitzgerald, and Kinney sat in the back row of a packed house. The audience was so utterly engaged and inspired by Frisell's masterful jazz guitar playing that a realization dawned on each of them at almost the very same time. "This is church!" From that point on, they began to think of how they might do church differently, more dialogically in ways that connected with folks outside the church.

In 2009 Kinney incorporated the Front Porch as a nonprofit and began hosting weekly events and conversations at Texas French Bread and the Spider House with a particular focus on the sustainable food culture in Austin. 2011 is when they became a parochial mission of All Saints. It began as a small batch gathering of like-minded souls. This small batch has grown in its understanding about its own mission as well as numerically as it has impacted life in the city of Austin.

By inviting people of all creeds to engage in their radically open understanding of Christ and communion, the Front Porch strives to become the go-to place for speaking openly about things that matter in an intentionally spiritual way that builds bridges among different outlooks. Right now they have four different programs or approaches for doing what they do.

The first of these is called Parable, which is basically a reimagined Sunday evening worship service. They outgrew their original space at the popular Opal Divine's, a pub in South Austin, and moved to Scholz's beer garden, where they host fifty to one hundred people each time they meet. While about half of these people are becoming regulars, they also notice that the other half come and go out of curiosity or word of mouth or because they know the musicians or their guests. Most are not attending church anywhere or have slacked off from churchgoing. They used to meet once per month, but starting in August 2015, they will gather weekly.

What happens? Folks gather and order food and drink around 5:30 p.m., while a local band or musician plays bluegrass, jazz, classical, or folk. At 5:45 p.m., they welcome everybody and orient their attention with some mindful silence and a prayer. Their musicians then play something original or lead in singing something together, secular or sacred. It's very informal and ad-libbed. Then they introduce their invited guest or a thinker-in-residence and conduct a twenty-minute conversation on a topic of their choice. To give access to distinguished and interesting Austinites, they teamed up with NPR's John Burnett, who has led them into soulful conversations with some of Austin's great citizens, people like music legend Ray Benson, rabbi and jazz activist Neil Blumofe, public advocate and gardener Tom Spencer, state senator Kirk Watson, writer and activist Ellen Sweets, Austin foodie and restaurateur Jessie Griffiths, *Edible Austin* publisher Marla Camp, speaker and therapist J. Pittman McGehee, *Texas Tribune* editor Evan Smith, entrepreneur Turk Pipkin, homeless advocate and director of Foundation Communities Walter Moreau, naturalist Victor Emanuel, and so many others. Each of these guests brings a unique perspective to the porch that, in turn, attracts interesting new people. Some of whom keep coming. At the least, each perspective generates a fifteen-minute follow-up conversation with everybody in attendance.

After the open-ended conversation time, they play more music or sing something else together, while they set the table for their rather unique communion service, where they recover the idea and practice of table fellowship with Jesus, who had the habit of eating with sinners. This is a relatively short but meaningful and even joyful time. Many folks may attend Parable for the celebrity guests or great music, but they are finding that this communion service is fast becoming the real heart and soul of their gathering. They tag it as communion, not religion, in an effort to get folks rethinking their preconceived notions of what it means to be Christian in a culture that has co-opted and confused the vocabulary and meaning of Christianity itself.

Their second program, Unplugged on the Front Porch, occurs every third Thursday of each month in the acoustically perfect All Saints sanctuary. They've teamed up with another Austin nonprofit, the Live Music Capital Foundation, to welcome folks into beautiful sacred space for concerts and conversations with Austin's most notable storytellers and musicians.[133]

They've received overwhelmingly positive responses from audiences, which range from 75 to 175 in size. The artists play an hour and a half of music for an audience over two musical sets. These sets are divided by a revealing, fifteen-minute interview with Steve Kinney, which provides the musicians a new opportunity to tell previously unheard parts of their story. All Saints sacred space works its magic to influence the evening; inevitably there is a reverential experience of art that calls everybody into a spiritually deeper place that often inspires people to learn more about the Front Porch and All Saints church.

By allowing the universal language of music to connect us, the audience connects directly with the musician and each other through the shared experience. Unplugged also cross-fertilizes the Front Porch by bringing new types of folks onto the porch each month, those who may not be coming to their other events.

Their third track of programming is called Elephant in the Room. They are in the process of rebranding this track. The idea of Elephant in the Room is to bring folks together from all over Austin around interesting, relevant cultural topics to engage them dialogically and to develop their solution-focused conversation skills. With help from informed and personable moderators, they facilitate discussion about what otherwise might be taboo subjects. Their most recent event featured Michael Morton, whose award-winning film, *An Unreal Dream*, was screened for a diverse, packed audience at the Alamo Draft House, where they then moderated a public conversation about restorative justice and forgiveness.

A few months earlier, they hosted a symposium with Becca Stevens, director of Magdalene House and Thistle Farms, to focus on the rise of human trafficking in Austin and explore ways to end it. They collaborated on this well-attended event with other partners to address a common need, including Allies Against Slavery, St. David's Episcopal Church, Texas Council on Family Violence, and many others.

They are expanding and rebranding this third track to include all the other special events they do. Right now, for example, they are in the process of launching a new monthly series called Film Church. They are partnering on this with the Alamo Draft House and the Cultural Leadership Project "to champion the best filmmakers at the forefront of cultural change to help edify and enrich the spirit of culture and community." The idea here is to host and curate a one-hour conversation at the theater that follows the screening of whichever independent film Alamo Draft House has recommended for that month. They hope to acknowledge and humanize the spiritual and cultural significance of the theatergoing experience by providing a unique model for film discussion that builds a sense of community around a favored pastime, while also enabling Austin moviegoers to assess and better understand the films they choose to see.

This third track also encompasses various other Front Porch events that they produce and host under their brand. This includes a weekly businessmen's Bible study, an annual fall lecture series at All Saints, and the annual Lenten program also held at All Saints but produced by the Front Porch. This track also includes the unique events that get put together as a need arises. This fall, for example, they are hosting and moderating a benefit concert with the celebrated Austin musician, Gina Chavez, to help give voice to and raise money for a small, local nonprofit that we've become friends with. It's called Conspire, and they reach out to women in prison through art and drama.

Our fourth track of programming is called the Window, which hopes to provide a model for doing youth-led, cutting-edge outreach to the community of Austin. The Window, led by Kinney's twenty-three-year-old assistant, Riley Webb, builds community through shared outreach experience and dialogue with youth aged eleven to eighteen so these young people gain a deeper sense of their own identity and purpose while also calling others in the community-at-large into significant and frequent opportunities to love their neighbors.

Over the years, they have learned the following:

- Community is built one conversation at a time, and this requires lots of patience, persistence, coffee, and beer.
- The vision and mission of the Front Porch is very difficult to pin down, but it has to be articulated more clearly and simply, and lots of money has to be raised to sustain it.
- They have to "go with the givens," that is, it's not about results per se but about the arduous process of working together for a common purpose. This takes time.
- People outside the church can be very suspicious of the church. They need lots of reassurance that we are not a bait-and-switch project. Are we?
- The church needs to rethink its modern view of truth-as-objective more in terms of a postmodern, relational view of truth.
- The self is not a substance in and of itself but an integrity that one must struggle to bring into existence over time through the labor of ongoing exchange in dialogue.
- Dialogue with and among others is a lost art in our smartphone-mediated, yet conversation-deficit, culture that prizes tribal collectives based on similarities or ideology.
- People want to share their hard-won perspective, and they have lots to say, if given the chance and time.
- When the need for different voices is affirmed and experienced, a higher-order unity emerges among people in the group that is always greater than the sum of its parts.
- Dialogue works best when virtues of vulnerability, openness, humility, and trust are in the mix. This takes time and vulnerability.
- Dialogue flourishes when things are messy and even in tension. Unfortunately not everybody can tolerate or appreciate messiness and chaos.

The Front Porch has emerged from the bottom-up, so to speak. So things have happened in a very organic, open-ended fashion, literally one conversation at a time. There have been thousands of different iterations, ideas, and interactions that have contributed to what it has become. So it's hard to look back and think how he would have done it differently without messing up what they have now. Kinney says,

But if I could have done it differently, knowing what I now know, I would've allied myself with a more practically minded partner than the fellow idealist partner that I had in the beginning. Then again, my idealist partner was the one who kept me dreaming about possibilities. But, she was too much like myself, and I needed someone with a more outcome-minded skillset. Also, I would've given up earlier on the vision that we were going to grow into our own physical space. While I still think it would be great to have our own space, I now realize that such a goal was unrealistic for that time and that I spent too much time worrying about how to achieve that instead of focusing on what I could do within my own limitations and gifts.

Further Recommendations for Reading

If Jesus Were Mayor by Bob Moffitt

Barefoot Church by Brandon Hatmaker

Missional Renaissance: Changing the Scorecard for the Church by Reggie McNeal

Missional: Joining God in the Neighborhood by Alan Roxburgh

Get Off Your Donkey: Help Someone and Help Yourself by Reggie McNeal

Peppermint Filled Piñatas by Eric Michael Bryant

The Secular Age and Sources of the Self by Charles Taylor

On Christian Theology by Rowan Williams

Problems of Dostoevsky's Poetics by Mikhail Bakhtin

Communion and Otherness by John Zizioulas

One, the Three, and the Many by Colin Gunton

The Brothers Karamazov by Fyodor Dostoevsky

Chapter 11

Frequently Asked Questions

Are small batch communities and missional communities the same thing?

Yes. The terms are interchangeable.

What is a small batch/missional community?

A small batch/missional community is a different way of being church in the VUCA world. We define a missional community as a group of people about the size of an extended family sent into the world to live as missionaries so they might serve a specific people group.

What does VUCA mean again?

VUCA stands for volatility, uncertainty, complexity, and ambiguity. It is a way of describing our missionary context.

What do you mean by a "people group"?

A small batch community does not have a vague call to serve the world in general. Rather they focus on blessing and serving a particular group of people. A people group can be anyone, for example, residents that fall within a geographic area (a neighborhood, prison, nursing home, or apartment complex), students at a university, teachers at an elementary school, and so forth.

Is missional synonymous with "emerging?"

No. There are many good things happening in the church today that fall under the category of emerging church. Small batch is not necessarily one of them. Missional communities are not a newcomer program or even a cutting-edge plan to grow our traditional congregations. They are a new way that we believe that God is asking us to incarnate ourselves in the VUCA world so we might be the body of Christ.

What do small batch communities value?

Risk-taking, multiplication, and service

What do they actually do?

They live as missionaries and apostles as they serve their people group, study the Bible, pray, and eat.

How many different forms can a missional community take?

As many as you can think of. As long as a group of people are connected to a sending church, they covenant together to live as missionaries in service to a specific people group, and they gather regularly to eat, pray, and study scripture. They are what we now call a missional community.

How does a missional community/small batch differ from a traditional church plant?

A church plant is one person sent out to start a new community. A missional community is a group of people sent out to be a community.

Can a missional community turn into a church plant?

It may happen, as missional communities take root and multiply, they discern the need for a new anchor church (a traditional church plant). However, the end game in starting new missional communities is not to plant churches, but to serve the world in Jesus's name.

So what exactly is the goal in starting small batch/missional communities?

We want our traditional Episcopal parishes to become sending churches that equip and send missionaries into the VUCA world as apostles to seek and serve Christ in all persons (or people groups).

Can a traditional church have more than one missional community?

Yes. Churches of every size can have multiple missional communities. We want our sending churches to sow small batch communities just as extravagantly and recklessly as the sower in Jesus's parable, which means we know that only some will take root and bear fruit.

Does a small batch community need to have a priest in it?

No, but it certainly can. A missional community can be led by a priest, deacon, or layperson.

In what ways are missional communities and sending churches different?

They are parallel ecclesiastical structures. The sending church is traditional, liturgical, and therefore slow to adapt. Its focus is to feed the body of Christ, that is, the church. The missional community, on the other hand, exists to be the functional body of Christ and to feed the world. It exists for no other purpose than to serve the world in Jesus's name. See the chart below.

The Sending Church	The Missional Community
Priestly–connects people to Jesus	Diaconal–connects Jesus to people
Discipleship	Apostleship
The Sower	The Seeds
The Vine	The Branches
Inwardly focused	Outwardly focused
Values growth (in numbers and depth)	Values service and multiplication
Vertical	Horizontal
Traditional	Adaptive
Eucharist	Agape Meal
Prayer shapes actions	Action shapes prayer
Meets Jesus in the Upper Room	Meets Jesus on the Road to Emmaus
Failure is threatening	Failure is expected
Teaching the Gospel to Law-abiding Jews	Reinterpreting the Gospel for the Gentiles
Celebrate / Receive the Sacrament	Enact / Become the Sacrament
Peter	Paul
Jerusalem	The Diaspora
Honors the Sabbath	Heals on the Sabbath
Washes hands before Sacrament	Washes feet *as* Sacrament

How are sending churches and missional communities related?

They exist as a posture of encouraging reciprocity. Missional communities reflect back to our sending churches our apostolic identity and our need to break tradition so we might hold to tradition. Our sending churches, on the other hand, reflect back to our missional communities our deep rootedness in some traditions that cannot change because they were instituted by Christ Himself.

Will forming missional communities be a break from our Episcopal tradition?

No. We are forming these communities to honor our Episcopal tradition that values equipping missionaries to serve the world in Jesus's name. In the VUCA world, living into our ancient tradition will mean equipping and sending people to plant these small batch churches. However, because they will break traditional ecclesiological rules, people may perceive them to break with our tradition. Like Jesus, they will break with tradition so they might honor tradition.

How will our sending churches equip missional communities?

Primarily through listening and presence. Our small batch leaders will learn on the road and reflect back to our sending churches their needs as they arise.

Can members of the small batch remain involved in their sending church?

The missional community is a church in and of itself. However, those people working in, for example, a small batch church in a prison on Saturdays may want to worship in their sending church on Sunday mornings. Each must discern his or her own relationship to his or her sending church.

How does a missional church serve their people group?

In whatever way they can. The only rule is be salt and light, and the only metric for success is people served and parties thrown.

If I want to form a small batch community from my church, what is the next step?

Internalize this vision, tinker with it, contextualize it, share it with others, and see if the Spirit stirs any hearts. Begin praying and brainstorming with those interested in living as apostles and being sent off campus. Make sure the rector/pastoral leader is part of the conversation. Take the staff of your sending church's blessing, and walk the road to Emmaus to encounter Jesus through the people you serve. Then tell us what you see, and teach us what you need so we can support you.

CHAPTER 12

COMMUNITIES OF INSPIRATION

Each of the small batch communities featured in this book offer inspiration about what others are doing across the Episcopal church. They too looked toward others and sought out fellow small batch pilgrims. Here is a list of communities and websites that might offer inspiration for you as you begin to take your first steps into the world of small batch:

- Creative Mornings, http://creativemornings.com/cities/atx
- Conversation Corps, http://atxtalks.org
- KUT's Brews and Views, http://kut.org/views-and-brews/#
- The Red Bench, http://interfaithtexas.org/dialogue/the-red-bench
- Conversation Cafés, http://www.conversationcafe.org
- Fremont Abbey, http://fremontabbey.org
- Strange Brew, http://www.strangebrewaustin.com
- Union Coffee House, http://uniondallas.net
- Space 12, http://www.space12.org
- Ebenezer's, http://ebenezerscoffeehouse.com
- Ignite Austin, http://www.igniteaustin.org
- Dionysium, http://www.dionysium.org
- Fusebox Festival, http://www.fuseboxfestival.com
- The Ark, http://www.theark.org
- Thad's, http://www.thads.org
- Freight and Salvage Coffeehouse, http://www.thefreight.org
- St. Julian's Episcopal Church, http://www.stjuliansaustin.org

- St. Mark's Between the Bayous, http://www.stmarks-houston.org/index.php?page=between-the-bayous
- Nadia Bolz Webber at House of All Sinners and Saints, http://www.houseforall.org
- Kerlin Richter's work at Bushwick Abbey, http://bushwickabbey.org
- Stephanie Spellers's work at the Crossing in Boston, http://www.thecrossingboston.org
- Solomon's Porch in Minneapolis, www.solomonsporch.com
- Slate Project, http://www.slateproject.org

Melissa Skelton's work at St. Paul's Seattle (http://www.stpaulseattle.org) was fundamentally missional. Sean Lannigan is just getting started. He is the pastor of Holy Ground in Long Beach, California (https://www.facebook.com/holygroundlbc?pnref=lhc). Erik Christiansen in Chicago is moving his traditional Lutheran Church to sell their building and start something yet to be determined at St. Luke's Logan Square (http://www.stlukesls.org). Tiffany Cheney in Boston is doing good work at the Intersection (http://www.connectingfaithandlife.org/Pages/default.aspx).

Chapter 13

Let There Be No Misunderstanding

The crowd came together again, so that they could not even eat. When his family heard it, they went out to restrain him, for people were saying, "He has gone out of his mind." And the scribes who came down from Jerusalem said, "He has Beelzebul, and by the ruler of the demons he casts out demons." And he called them to him, and spoke to them in parables, "How can Satan cast out Satan? If a kingdom is divided against itself, that kingdom cannot stand. And if a house is divided against itself, that house will not be able to stand. And if Satan has risen up against himself and is divided, he cannot stand, but his end has come. But no one can enter a strong man's house and plunder his property without first tying up the strong man; then indeed the house can be plundered. "Truly I tell you, people will be forgiven for their sins and whatever blasphemies they utter; but whoever blasphemes against the Holy Spirit can never have forgiveness, but is guilty of an eternal sin"—for they had said, "He has an unclean spirit." Then his mother and his brothers came; and standing outside, they sent to him and called him. A crowd was sitting around him; and they said to him, "Your mother and your brothers and sisters are outside, asking for you." And he replied, "Who are my mother and my brothers?" And looking at those who sat around him, he said, "Here are my mother and my brothers! Whoever does the will of God is my brother and sister and mother."

—Mark 3:20–35

There was once a church misunderstanding. I was travelling with a friend and talking about visiting All Saints Episcopal Church in Austin.

It was my birthday, and I was really excited to go to All Saints because you get a birthday blessing during the announcements. Here's the thing: you get to put money in a church-shaped birthday piggy bank.

It is amazing. They have this church-shaped piggy bank, and you put money in it. You are supposed to put a penny in for every year or a dollar if you are an adult. I was explaining how excited I was about going and getting to do this because I'm a church geek. My friend was telling me he was at All Saints for a while, and he really loved it there. But he remembers on his first Sunday there that all of the anxiety that flowed over him because, even though he'd been a lifelong Episcopalian, he'd never seen the church-shaped piggy bank for the birthday blessing. He tends to be a little bit of an anxious person, so he began to worry about what happens. Are you paying for the blessing? Then he began to ponder what would happen if it were his birthday and he didn't have any money. Could he still get a blessing? He was running through all of these scenarios. He had completely misunderstood the whole thing.

That got me thinking about this misunderstanding about the "birthday church," as I like to call it. And so I went and did a little bit of research because I wanted to know where the birthday church came from. I found out actually nobody at All Saints knows where the birthday church came from, typical of our church traditions. I did a little more research, and this is what I found out. I'm going to give you a little history.

Evidently in the Middle Ages (and that's where our story begins), coins were very precious. Yes, of course they were. Where would you want to put your coin? You'd want to put it in a protected place. People who were potters would make ceramic boxes with a little slit in the top so you could put your coin in the ceramic box. Now the box was named after the ceramic that was used, the clay that was used to make it, or "pyg." This is where the idea of a piggy bank comes from. Clever potters would make their pyg banks into the shape of a pig as a clever potter's pun.

Churches began to use the pyg at the front door because we didn't always do stewardship campaigns and all this other business. What you basically did was you came and put a coin in a pyg or money box. You put it in the church piggy bank. And of course, because craftsman are crafty, they also figured out they could make money in putting them in the shape of churches. And so over time, these ideas, these mite boxes (and some of you know about mite boxes) or little boxes were created, and they evolved into these different things, including the birthday church bank.

Interestingly the bank at All Saints has been around since the fifties and has paid for a roof and windows, and today it pays for outreach and ministry into the community. It's an interesting little story I discovered just out of a pure church misunderstanding.

I think one of the things that's important to know is that we are a church of traditions. I think it's important for us from time to time to reveal how people understand the church, to correct misunderstandings about tradition, and to help our people know what things are for and about. I think that's one of the primary roles that we undertake as Christians, preachers, and teachers in the church.

I want to offer this though. There was a great theologian, Emil Brunner. He is most well-known for a huge debate with another theologian, Karl Barth, but that's a whole other story altogether. Emil Brunner wrote *The Church Misunderstanding*. In it he proposed this idea, which I think is accurate. "Religion is always attempting to point towards God but it is always something that is bound by our human nature in the world and so is always a mere reflection of the ecclesia."[134]

Our context in this world is always the lens by which we see God. We can always and everywhere only glimpse the ecclesia or God's dream of what the church is to be, what the human family, we might say, is supposed to be. There's a difference between what God dreams for us and most oftentimes what we experience. And this reality, this misunderstanding, if you will, is exactly the kind of trouble we see in this gospel passage from Mark.

Jesus is a good religious boy. He has made pilgrimages. He's probably offered sacrifices and all that's required of him by the faith of his day. He probably—and we truly believe this—went oftentimes to services where they would read the scripture. Some people even believed he probably studied a little bit of the scripture, the Old Testament, to be particular. He was a good religious boy.

But in our passage today, what we find is that he's gone crazy. Jesus is nuts. That's what it says. What happens is his family hears that Jesus is nearby and all these people are there. They're going to go see him, and when they arrive, the people say, "This is the way things work in the world, and Jesus is upsetting the apple cart." The people come to the parents to get them to do something about their child Jesus. Some things haven't changed much in two thousand years. They go to Jesus's parents, and they say, "He's crazy, this guy. He's saying and doing things that just don't make a whole lot of sense, and you've got to put a stop to it. You've got to stop him."

I think there are four things Jesus is teaching that are clear in the scripture. Let there be no misunderstanding.

1. One of the things he is doing is healing people outside of the religion of the day. At that time, to be healed, you had to go and

offer a sacrifice at the temple. Jesus is having none of that. He's just wandering around the countryside healing people. He's healing them and restoring them, all kinds of people. It's not the way things are done, these people say.
2. He's preaching outside of the religious sites. He's not going to the places where teaching normally happens. He's standing out in the open, talking to people. That's wrong, they say. You've got to stop that. Jesus is doing things incorrectly.
3. He's hanging out with people that religious people don't like to hang out with. That seems to be causing a lot of heartburn. He's a good religious boy, but he's not hanging out with the right people. Can you imagine poor Mary having to listen to all this? Jesus is hanging out with people with whom the religious authorities believe are unclean and not worthy of community. They have 617 rules about how that is true.
4. Jesus is redefining what faithfulness means. To follow God—whom he calls Father—or follow Jesus is different than all of the religious stuff you've been given, he offers.

The people want him to stop. I want to say to you, "Clearly I think this is why Jesus was killed." I really think he was killed because he is undermining society in every form, and everybody who has any stake in society needs to get this man to be quiet. I think it's because Jesus is very clear and there can be no misunderstanding.

He offers some pieces about faithfulness to us. We human beings are actually responsible, according to Jesus, for one another. That's part of what it means to be family, that is, we're responsible for one another. We're responsible for carrying and healing people and for feeding, clothing, and housing one another. God created all of these things, and there's enough to go around. And Jesus teaches us we are to be about that business. That's the work we're supposed to do.

There's a great moment in the scripture when he meets a woman at the well. Some of you know this story. And she says to him something like, "Well, I've heard you're supposed to either worship God on this mountain over here, or you're supposed to go to these holy sites and worship him over there." Jesus says (and I am paraphrasing), "No, that's not true. When people worship God, this God I'm teaching you about, and this spirit and truth, then people will be worshipping this God out in the world. People will take their altars outside, out into the world. God will be worshipped there in the midst of their relationships."

Faithfulness is not always found in the inherited temples of our day. Jesus tells us that we are always more clearly the family of God when we are hanging out with people who are different than us, that is, when we're eating with them or listening to them, just being with them.

Jesus says to be faithful is to really make God and God's family—our brothers and sisters, our neighbors, and our community—at the center of our lives. And that's what religion is about. That's what God's dream of his family is about. Let there be no misunderstanding that, when we are at our best, we who make religion are always reflecting more on this dream that God has of his family than the ideas that we have about church.

Everything we have—all of our resources, gifts, talents, energies, buildings, and structures as a church—is to be used for these things. That's the truth. Everything is to be directed at bringing about this family that God dreams about. Where our church does not do these things, it is our responsibility to reform it. It's our responsibility.

Remember what Jesus said about the strong man? The strong man must be tied up. We are invited to bind up our natural inclination to have it our way. We are to bind up our idea of church about the way it used to be and the way it's supposed to be. We're to bind up all of those powers that we get out of running church this way. We are to bind up our desires to protect and preserve something at times that does not reflect what God intends. And I would offer that Jesus in that parable about the strong man is actually inviting us to plunder the church house, that is, all of its resources might be put to the creation of God's family. After all, this is what it means to be part of the Jesus movement, to do everything we can to share the gospel and create a Christian community.

Let there be no misunderstanding about church. And let us honor the fact that this makes us nervous. I don't know about you. Many of you are like, "Let's go! We're selling it! You're the last one to worship here." Not really of course. It should make us nervous. It should. It's intended to provoke us.

What I know is that, in your heart, you know when we're at our best. This is what we do. You know I'm not lying to you. You know, just like I do, this is what God intends. You and I have been called to this moment. We have been called to this time. We're the ones who get to write the history of the church in this era. We're the ones who get to pass on what this church does in the world to the next generation. I think in our hearts we want to write a church story that's a little closer, a little more like what God wants for us, so there is an understanding of who God is and how He cares, loves, and forgives. At the core of that vision is the small batch Christian community. A return to a local, organic, and sustainable model of mission is in sync with Jesus's vision of Christian community. That, my friends, I believe is a church worth working for.

Dispatches from the Front: The SoCo

Let me introduce to you the SoCo community of Austin, Texas. It is a house church concept started by lay leader and now postulant for holy orders, Paul Skeith. St. David's is the sending church. Since January 2015, their Sunday service averages about fifteen people each Sunday. The community has a core group of about seven regulars who attend almost every week, including the founding leader's family, and about forty other members come to a Sunday service off and on and on holidays. Community members range in age from age eight to eighty, including children, married couples, and single people. Out of the current members, about a third are Latino, and about two-thirds are white. They have several LGBT folks who attend. *This is their story.*

The SoCo Episcopal Community worships and serves their neighbors in Austin, Texas, in the 78704 zip code, ground zero of "Keep Austin Weird." "SoCo" refers to South Congress Avenue, and the surrounding area has come to be known as "SoCo" in the last ten years. South Congress is lined with funky shops, restaurants, bars, boutique hotels, and food trucks, and it has become an entertainment destination for both Austinites and out-of-town visitors. Neighborhood home prices and apartment rents have at least doubled in the last ten years, but there are also public, subsidized, older, and low-income apartments in the area as well. The large majority of students in every SoCo area school are Latino and members of low-income families. The total number of children living in the SoCo area has decreased in the last ten years as the neighborhood has become less affordable, and many smaller, older churches in the neighborhood have shrunk in numbers and closed as their members have died or moved to the suburbs looking for a more affordable place to live. My sense from talking with neighbors is that a significant majority of people now living in the SoCo area are not connected to a religious congregation or are only marginally connected to a congregation.

How It Began

The SoCo Episcopal Community began after Skeith's family moved back into their house in the SoCo neighborhood after hopping from friend's house to friend's house for six months during a remodel. They wanted to celebrate moving back home, and they asked The Reverend David Boyd, then the rector of St. David's Episcopal Church, if he would come and bless the house. Paul's wife Minerva was very involved in the Hispanic Outreach Ministry in Evangelism Group, the "Homies," at St. David's at the time. The Homies were trying to plan a Eucharist to celebrate the feast of Our Lady of Guadalupe on December 12, 2013, which happened to fall on a Thursday evening that year. The problem was that St. David's was normally closed Thursday evenings, and it would involve asking a lot of people to come to work to make the Eucharist happen at St. David's that night. Minerva and David talked about it, and they decided they would combine their house blessing and the Our Lady of Guadalupe Eucharist. About forty people came to celebrate, and Minerva and Paul noticed that many of the people who came were neighbors who were not connected to any religious congregation or even any religious tradition.

Together they wondered what it would be like if they started having a service in their house and invited their friends, family, and neighbors who identified themselves as religious "nones" but were curious about the spiritual dimension of life. They talked with David Boyd about it, and he said, "Great, yes! Go do it!" David also said it sounded like a satellite church idea that I had invited St. David's to explore.

So starting in January 2014, Skeith began gatherings in their house one Saturday afternoon a month for evening prayer followed by a potluck dinner. For Easter that year, they attempted a full Easter vigil service at the house, complete with the lighting of the new fire in a hibachi in their front yard. About twenty-five people came, and based on that turnout, they decided it was time to start meeting twice a month, still on Saturday afternoons. This continued through the summer and fall of 2014.

On Christmas Eve, they had about forty-five people come to the house for a fantastic Christmas Eve service and party. While they were cleaning up that night and preparing for their family gathering the next day, they looked at each other and decided two things:

1. If the community were going to take on a real life of its own, they needed to get together every week.
2. There was no way they could still have the service in their house and not get divorced! So they had to rethink their start-up.

Minerva and Paul started calling local restaurants on South Congress that had a separate room to see if they would host the community. A few said yes until they realized it was a church that wanted to use their backroom and buy their tacos and beer. Then they heard something like, "We don't think we would be a good fit because we sometimes need to use the room on Saturday night/Sunday morning/Sunday evening."

The fifth establishment they approached was a bar called Opal Divine's Penn Field, who had previously hosted the Front Porch. Front Porch had outgrown the space, and Opal Divine's was happy and gracious enough to host their little group on Sunday afternoons. Opal's was pretty slow on Sunday afternoons, and they allowed them to use the room without charge as long as they stayed to eat and drink after the service, which they were happy to do. Because of this, their services moved from Saturday afternoons to Sunday afternoons.

Since they were trying to move the service out of the house, the Skeiths realized they would likely need money to make this happen and get out the word about the community. They talked with David Boyd and Terry Nathan, St. David's parish administrator, and set up a designated fund for the community that St. David's staff would manage. Minerva and Paul made an initial contribution to the designated fund, and the St. David's vestry also made a financial commitment to the community in the parish budget for 2015. They also started putting out a tip jar at each of their services to collect cash donations without saying much about it. They currently collect about thirty to fifty dollars a week from the tip jar. All in all, they projected that they could operate the community with an annual budget of five thousand dollars per year, which seems about right given their current operations. Of course the meal payments at Opal Divine's currently subsidize their space, and their best guess is that people attending their services will wind up spending a collective total of an additional five thousand dollars in food and drink through the end of the year. They are hopeful they can have enough regulars willing to autopay ten dollars a week through PayPal to cover all of the community's operating expenses by the end of 2016.

About this same time, Skeith created a Facebook page for the SoCo Episcopal Community, signed up for a SoCo Episcopal Community-branded Gmail address, purchased a logo for the community through the website Fiver, procured a Meetup subscription, and bought a monthly subscription for a template website, contact management, and online donation system called NationBuilder. He began to create Facebook events for each of their services and service outings. He also boldly friended everyone he had ever met and invited them to the SoCo events and asked them to have coffee. He also put together a brief e-mail newsletter that he sent out about once a week with announcements and upcoming events. He tried to send out three individual check-in e-mails a week to community regulars and those who have expressed some interest in the community.

He also tries to have at least one individual meeting with a regular or an interested at least once a week.

> The invitations to the coffee meetings usually go something like this,
>
> > I know this might not be your thing, but I am looking for people who are connected to the neighborhood to talk with about what is going on in the area. I am not trying to convert you or save you, and it's totally fine if you say no, but I would really like to get your perspective on what is going on.

If someone accepts his invitation for coffee, he talks about their interests, background, family, and what is going on in the neighborhood. For about two-thirds of the folks he meets with, the conversation stops there. Some of the people he meets with, however, are curious about what they are trying to accomplish or what he is up to. He often explains they are trying to build a real community in the neighborhood that plugs in and serves other existing neighborhood institutions like schools and a local nursing home. He also says they are an Episcopal faith community, but they don't care what people believe. Everyone is welcome. If they are curious and want to be part of what they do, which is prayer in the Episcopal Christian tradition, service to their neighbors, and working for God's justice in our city, they invite them to come and join SoCo and see if they are a good fit.

What They Are Learning and Trying

Skeith believes they wasted a lot of time in the first few months of 2015 creating complete printed worship bulletins and music each week. This process usually took several hours to accomplish, even using online tools like RiteWorship. In retrospect, instead of spending time working on bulletins, he should have spent that time meeting and talking with people interested in the community. When he ran out of time and energy, he just threw out the bulletins altogether and instead handed out Books of Common Prayer and announced page numbers. It worked just fine. And he got three hours of his life back each week.

Their services in the bar look surprisingly traditional. The community normally sets up worship space choir style with two rows of chairs facing each other, a table as an altar at one end set with candles and a seasonal color cloth, and a tall, round bar table serving as an lectern at the other end. They mostly sing Taizé songs from a small books and hymns from the hymnal without instrumental accompaniment. They say or sing the Psalms antiphonally to each other, and last Advent they chanted the Psalms using the Plainsong Psalter. The Reverend Carol Petty celebrates Eucharist with them once a month as their sacramentalist, and on the other Sundays they celebrate a Liturgy of the Word, and Paul preaches.

They also schedule times when they go together as the community to serve their neighbors. So far they have helped people wash and dry cloths as part of St. David's Laundry Love that takes place Thursday evenings at a Laundromat on South Congress near Opal Divine's. They have also gotten muddy working to clean up a local creek and pull invasive plants, and they have served food and worshipped with homeless neighbors at the Trinity Center in nearby downtown Austin.

While he typically does not wear vestments when they are having their normal service at the bar, he almost always wears vestments when they are worshipping in public so people can see that the church still exists. Last fall they held their evening service and blessed dogs and humans on Feast of St. Francis in a local off-leash dog park. One of the men in the park was tattooed in almost every place one could imagine having a tattoo, supplemented with multiple piercings and bars in various places. When he put on a cassock and surplice, however, it was clear that he was the scary, weird one in the park, and the man walked away, giving him as much room as possible. Fortunately the dogs did not mind the vestments, and a number of community members went around asking people in the park if they wanted their dogs blessed. Almost all said yes, and they handed them a card explaining who they were and what they were doing and invited them to join SoCo for their next service.

On Ash Wednesday this year, Minerva, his son Augustin, and Paul went out to the sidewalk in front of a little park on the same street as his son's elementary school with a sign that said "Ashes to Go." Ashes to Go is something that St. David's had done for several years in downtown Austin, and they thought they would try it in the SoCo neighborhood. Amazingly about forty cars pulled over during the hour they stood on the street, and they imposed ashes on well over eighty people, mostly Latinos who lived in the nearby apartments. While some of the folks who pulled over felt connected to a church, the vast majority had no relationship with a church at all. They gave people who were interested a little flyer inviting them to look at their website and come to services.

In addition to spending time in the physical space of the neighborhood, he is trying to learn how to effectively use the web and mobile devices to provide people with the tools they need to satisfy their hunger for an experience of God and connection with authentic community. He has just started to spend a few hours a week writing short comments and curating books, audio programs, and videos about the church, Christianity, theology, service, social justice, parenting, prayer, and the spiritual life. He has been publishing these materials on the community's webpage (www.socoepiscopal.org) and through the community's Facebook, Google+, Twitter, and Instagram accounts. He posts audio files of his sermons through these same social media channels. Using their contact management system, they also sent out a short e-mail each week that reminds everyone to come to the service and lets everyone know what is new that week.

Most recently they have been experimenting with praying morning prayer together at 8:00 a.m. on Wednesday mornings by using Google Hangouts, a free video conference service. So far a few community folks have tried this, but several have been frustrated by trying to make the technology work.

In the next few months, the biggest challenge the community will face is to transition leadership and responsibility for various parts of the operations of the community more broadly among the members of the community according to their passions and talents. They are blessed to have several strong leaders, but they will need to find more leaders to grow the community beyond what it is now. The plan is to start holding small group meetings to identify leaders and their interests in the early fall of 2015.

Paul is also personally challenged by the amount of time and emotional effort that trying to get the community off the ground is costing him while he is also trying to be a husband and dad, run his law practice, and try to finish up his studies at the Iona School for Ministry. He has had to really pay attention to his own mental and physical health and energy levels and be disciplined about taking time away from both work and the community for vacation, retreat, and just plain downtime. He also realizes how crucial the help of his administrative assistant at work has been to free up enough time to allow him to work on organizing the community. He would not be able to spend time on the things that really need to get done if he did not have her support. He also depends on advice from a business coach, a therapist who works with organizational leaders, and a spiritual director to help keep him on the rails.

Questions

1. What are some things that Jesus routinely did that today's church might call "crazy"? What often prevents us from being crazy like Jesus was?
2. Bishop Doyle reminds us that Jesus frequently healed people outside the religion of the day. Where do you see people being healed in

today's world outside of mainstream Christianity? Do you believe the Holy Spirit is at work outside of our church traditions?
3. What does it mean for us to be responsible for one another? What do you believe is your chief responsibility as a Christian?
4. How would you define the dream of God? How does the church often protect traditions at odds with God's dream? Which of our traditions best reflect God's dream?

Recommendations for Further Reading

Blessed Are the Organized: Grassroots Democracy in America by Jeffrey Stout.

Ernesto Cortes on Relational Meetings, https://www.youtube.com/watch?v=g42mLGATG-c

The E-Myth Revisited: Why Most Small Businesses Don't Work and What to Do About It by Michael E. Gerber

The Happiness Advantage: The Seven Principles of Positive Psychology That Fuel Success and Performance at Work by Shawn Achor

Pastrix: The Cranky, Beautiful Faith of a Sinner & Saint by Nadia Bolz-Weber

The Tipping Point: How Little Things Can Make a Big Difference by Malcolm Gladwell

About the Author

The Right Reverend C. Andrew Doyle, the ninth bishop of the Episcopal Diocese of Texas, summarizes his autobiography in six words: "Met Jesus on pilgrimage; still walking." He is author of *Generous Community*, *CHURCH*, *Unabashedly Episcopalian*, *Orgullosamente Episcopal*, and *Unity in Mission*. He and his wife JoAnne live in Houston with their daughters.

Endnotes

1. You can find the text of "On the Babylonian Captivity of the Church" here, http://whitehorsemedia.com/docs/BABYLONIAN_CAPTIVITY_OF_THE_CHURCH.pdf. It is written by the reformer Martin Luther.
2. Thomas S. Kuhn, *The Structure of Scientific Revolution* (Chicago: University of Chicago Press, 1996).
3. Ibid.
4. Brené Brown, *Daring Way Training* (February 2015).
5. Ronald A. Heifetz, *Leadership without Easy Answers* (Cambridge: The Belknap Press of University Press, 1994), 128.
6. Phillips Brooks, "Going up to Jerusalem" Twenty Sermons (1886), 330.
7. The Reverend Steve Kinney is priest in charge of the Front Porch, a missional community of All Saints Episcopal Church in Austin. They are fond of saying that they are "local, organic, and sustainable."
8. Emily Scott participated in a brief e-mail conversation and helped my research by answering a questionnaire. Her responses are offered here.
9. Nassim Nicholas Taleb, *The Black Swan: The Impact of the Highly Improbable* (New York: Random House, 2007), 8.
10. Daniel Kahneman, *Thinking, Fast and Slow* (Canada: Doubleday, 2011), 87.
11. Ibid, 85.
12. Ibid, 86.
13. Ibid, 202.
14. Wayne Meeks, First Urban Christians (New Haven: Yale University Press, 1983), 76.
15. Ibid, 75.
16. Ibid, 77.
17. Ibid, 78.
18. Ibid, 80.
19. Ibid, 80.
20. Ibid, 82.
21. Ibid, 83.

22 The customary is a list of usual practices for a community.
23 Edward Foley, *From Age to Age: How Christians Have Celebrated the Eucharist* (Chicago: Liturgy Training Publications, 1991), 39.
24 Ibid, 63.
25 Ibid. 87.
26 Bill Bryson, *At Home: A Short History of Private Life* (New York: Doubleday, 2010), 322, 475ff.
27 Charles Taylor, *A Secular Age* (Cambridge: The Belknap Press of Harvard University Press, 2007), 775.
28 Ibid, 774.
29 Ibid, 542.
30 Ibid, 543.
31 Harvey Cox, *Religion in the Secular City: Toward a Postmodern Theology* (New York: Simon and Shuster, 1984), 159.
32 Capra, *Turning Point*, 96, 99, as quoted in Wheatley, *New Science*, 20.
33 Uri Friedman, "12 Maps That Changed the World," *The Atlantic*, http://www.theatlantic.com/international/archive/2013/12/12-maps-that-changed-the-world/282666/
34 Ibid.
35 Ibid.
36 Ibid.
37 Ibid.
38 Wheatley, *New Science*, 34.
39 Scott Bader-Saye, "Bonds of Affection: The Transformational Possibilities of a Platitude," *The Conference*, 2014. Also see C. S. Lewis, *The Four Loves* (New York: Houghton Mifflin Harcourt, 1991), 31ff. Bader-Saye introduced me to this idea that affection is a key ingredient to Christian communities.
40 Ibid.
41 Ibid.
42 "Political Polarization in American Public: Political Polarization and Personal Life," Pew Research Center, June 12, 2014, http://www.people-press.org/2014/06/12/section-3-political-polarization-and-personal-life/
43 Bader-Saye.
44 Ibid.
45 Ibid.
46 Ibid.
47 Wendell Berry, "It All Turns on Affection," Awards and Honors: 2012 Jefferson Lecture, http://www.neh.gov/about/awards/jefferson-lecture/wendell-e-berry-lecture.
48 Marina Gorbis, *The Nature of the Future: Dispatches from the Socialstructed World* (New York: Free, 2013), 74.
49 Ibid.
50 Ibid, 176.
51 Scott Claasen participated in a brief e-mail conversation and helped my research by answering a questionnaire. His responses are offered here.

52 "Smart Cities and Smart Citizens," *Sustain Magazine*, May 1, 2013, http://sustainmagazine.com/smart-cities-smart-citizens.
53 Ibid.
54 Ibid.
55 Ibid.
56 Smart citizens live in smart cities. This is a way of networking people into a platform that generates participatory community life. Smart citizens are connected with one another and the population within a city. For example, the Amsterdam Smart City Project seeks to connect government officials, citizens, and academics to build government e-services.
57 Ibid.
58 Ibid.
59 Ibid.
60 Ibid.
61 Here is more information about Paul Baran on the Rand website. Paul worked for Rand Corporation, which used to be focused on military solutions. Today Rand is a firm doing analysis and consulting. http://www.rand.org/about/history
62 Ibid.
63 Ibid.
64 Ibid. See the actual report here, http://www.rand.org/content/dam/rand/pubs/research_memoranda/2006/RM3764.pdf.
65 Ibid.
66 Stuart Brand, "Founding Father, " *Wired*, September 2003, http://archive.wired.com/wired/archive/9.03/baran_pr.html
67 Ibid.
68 Katie Rengers participated in a brief e-mail conversation and helped my research by answering a questionnaire. His responses are offered here.
69 Nassim Nicholas Taleb, *Black Swan* (New York: Random House, 2007), 8.
70 A procrustean bed is a standard that is enforced uniformly without regard to individuality. Procrustes was a mythological figure who cut people down to size to fit in an iron bed.
71 Nassim Nicholas Taleb, *Antifragile: Things That Gain from Disorder* (New York: Random House, 2012), 106.
72 Modeled after diagram in Robert Johansen, *Leaders Make the Future: Ten New Leadership Skills for an Uncertain World* (San Francisco: Berrett-Koehler, 2012), 16.
73 Paul Baran, August 1964. You can find some of the graphs here, http://www.rand.org/about/history/baran.html
74 This cycle of innovation graph is taken from the National Science Foundation website here, http://www.nsf.gov/pubs/2009/nsf09506/nsf09506.htm.
75 Marina Gorbis, *The Nature of the Future*, 62.
76 Ibid.
77 Gorbis, 62. Gorbis writes, "Elizabeth Dunn, a professor of psychology, and her colleagues at the University of British Columbia showed that spending

more of one's income on others predicted greater happiness. Dunn's studies also show that participants who were randomly assigned to spend money on others experienced greater happiness than those assigned to spend money on themselves. Her work and other studies suggest that beyond the point at which people have economic security, happiness doesn't scale with money, even very large amounts of money. We are more happy spending money on social experiences than on buying things."

78 Gorbis, 64.
79 Caesar Kalinowski quote
80 David Peters participated in a brief e-mail conversation and helped my research by answering a questionnaire. His responses are offered here.
81 I began using the word "attractional church" in 2014. I am not sure where I gleaned the idea from. In 2015 I found a book called *Launching Missional Communities: A Field Guide* by Mike Breenard and Alex Absalom. In it is a similar chapter and a more Protestant view of the difference between a missional and attractional church. It is a book worth the read.
82 Caesar Kalinowski has a number of really good books. They are *Small is Big, Fast is Slow* and *Be The Church*. He is also willing to help coach new communities into existence. I brought him in to speak so others could hear about the amazing work that is going on out in the nondenominational world. He was a great speaker and inspiring.
83 George Barna and Mark Hatch, *Boiling Point: It Only Takes One Degree: Monitoring Cultural Shifts in the 21st Century* (Ventura, Calif.: Regal, 2001), 250.
84 Ibid, 252.
85 SimCity was a popular game that allowed people to build communities online.
86 Ibid, 251.
87 Flash mob Eucharist is a large public gathering where people have a Eucharist organized by means of social networks.
88 Ibid, 25. The Barna Group calls these boutique churches, "These are congregations with one ministry: worship, discipleship, fellowship, community service."
89 Ibid, 252.
90 Learn more about Episcopal Service Corps here, http://episcopalservicecorps.org.
91 Barna, *Boiling Point*, 252.
92 Ibid.
93 Ibid, 253.
94 Ibid, 253.
95 Bob Johansen, *Get There Early* (San Francisco: Berrett-Koehler, 2007), 21.
96 Institute for the Future, "2008–2018 Map of Future Forces Affecting the Episcopal Church," Presented at the Consortium of Endowed Parishes meeting at St. David's Episcopal Church, Austin, Texas, 2008.

97 Angie Thurston and Casper ter Kuile, "How We Gather," https://caspertk.wordpress.com/2015/04/18/how-we-gather-a-new-report-on-non-religious-community, April 18, 2015.
98 Ibid.
99 Ibid.
100 Ibid.
101 Ibid.
102 Thesanctuaries.org
103 Ibid.
104 The following qualities are taken from the guideposts that Brené Brown offers in her book, *Daring Greatly*. Brené Brown, *Daring Greatly: How the Courage to Be Vulnerable Transforms the Way We Live, Love, Parent, and Lead* (New York: Gotham, 2012), 10.
105 Ibid.
106 Ibid, 11.
107 Ibid.
108 Ibid.
109 Ibid, 244.
110 Ibid.
111 Ibid.
112 Ibid.
113 Ibid.
114 Ibid.
115 While I was working on this book, the Reverend Matt Moreno share some values he and a provincial team had come up with. In reflection about the commonalities I experienced through conversation with our diverse small batch ministries, I believe they share similar values. I have used the list Moreno gave me to organize my thoughts here.
116 Luc-Normand Tellier, *Urban World History* (Québec: Press de l'Université du Québec, 2009), 274.
117 Philip Smith Dictionary of Greek and Roman Biography and Mythology, s.v. "St. Ambrosius" (Boston: Little, Brown and Company, 1867), 139–140.
118 Craig Alan Satterlee, *Ambrose of Milan's Method of Mystagogical Preaching* (Collegeville, Mn: Liturgical Press, 2002), 47.
119 The Arian controversy describes several controversies between a one clergyman and theologian Arius and a bishop and Athanasius related to Christology. The controversy divided the church from before the Council of Nicaea in 325 to after the Council of Constantinople in 381. It dominated Church politics for over fifty years. It had to do with the nature of God, Jesus, and the Holy Trinity.
120 Smith.
121 Satterlee.
122 Paulinus, Vita Ambrossi, 9 (Novoni) 62. As quoted in Smith.
123 Read more about it here, http://www.anglicannews.org/news/2014/01/southern-africa-archbishop-launches-africa-e-reader-project.aspx.

124 L. Gregory Jones, "Something Old, Something New: Innovation in Theological Education," *Christian Century*, February 10, 2014, http://www.christiancentury.org/article/2014-01/something-old-something-new.
125 Ibid.
126 Ibid. Jones suggests for future reading, "Deep Trends Affecting Christian Institutions" by L. Gregory Jones and Nathan Jones at faithandleadership.com, http://www.faithandleadership.com/content/l-gregory-jones-and-nathan-jones-deep-trends-affecting-christian-institutions.
127 Ibid.
128 Gorbis, 133. Adapted.
129 Caesar Kalinowski.
130 Caesar Kalinowski said, "Slow if fast, small is big."
131 You can find the online article here, http://bushwickdaily.com/2014/01/church-that-doesnt-suck-an-abbey-of-christian-worship-grows-in-radio-bushwick.
132 Kerlin Richter participated in a brief e-mail conversation and helped my research by answering a questionnaire. His responses are offered here.
133 Mother Falcon, Sam Baker, Guy Forsyth, Darden Smith, Jimmie Dale Gilmore, Terri Hendrix and Lloyd Maines, Tish Hinojosa, Michael Fracasso, Sara Hickman, Eliza Gilkyson, Walt Wilkins, Ray Benson, Ruby Jane, Nelo, John Pointer, Will Taylor, Erin Ivey, and others.
134 Emil Brunner, *The Church Misunderstanding* (Philadelphia: Westminster, 1953), 115.

p. 43 - Mission Amplification — team approach — using collaboration + coaching to build cooperative + focused ministries in tandem.
— over time will give way for emerging natural networks that will live, sustain, + pass away as needed —

p. 53 - Small Batch = Stand alone — not tied to the 'hub'
p. 54 - Small Batch = local, sustainable, organic
p. 56 - the Small Batch Missional community forms people first thru service, as opposed to program/liturgy —

p. 63 - Small batch defined further — the ministry grows out of the organic life shared, Evangelism is exemplified (not taught), Formation is explored, Membership follows Service —
Friendlier to LGBTQ —

p. 21 - Author + Economist - Wendell Berry

Made in the USA
Lexington, KY
10 May 2017